The Dog-Nose Chronicles

The Dog-Nose Chronicles

A Sporting Novel

by

Cliff Hauptman

WILLOW CREEK PRESS

Minocqua, Wisconsin

Dedicated to the memories of
Richard Brautigan
Norman Maclean
Lee Wulff
and Ed Zern

Thanks for writing.
— C.H.

Portions of this book have appeared in slightly different forms in *Gray's Sporting
Journal* and *Fly Rod and Reel*.

Published by WILLOW CREEK PRESS
P.O. Box 147, Minocqua, WI 54548

For more information on other Willow Creek titles,
write or call 1-800-850-WILD.

Library of Congress Cataloging-in-Publication Data

Hauptman, Cliff
    The dog-nose chronicles : a sporting novel / Cliff Hauptman.
        p.   cm.
    ISBN 1-57223-084-3
    I. Title.
    PS3558.A7578D64   1997
    813'.54--dc21   97-1061
                                                                      CIP

Printed in the United States.

TABLE OF CONTENTS

Half the people can be part right all of the time,
And some of the people can be all right part of the time,
But all the people can't be all right all of the time.
I think Abraham Lincoln said that.
I'll let you be in my dream if I can be in yours.
I said that.

— Bob Dylan

Her name was Magill and she called herself Lil
But everyone knew her as Nancy.

— The Beatles

1
FOR THE RECORD

This is the end, my beautiful friend, the end.

— The Doors

Call me anything but Ishmael. It's a handle I ain't been able to live with since practically the day I was born. The whole litter of us kids were given Bible names by our mother, who was a regular fanatic on the subject. But I could never take to mine without getting the same feeling as when wearing horse-hair longjohns, and from nearly the beginning, most folks took to calling me Junior. I bring this up because in the book I am referred to as Ishmael and nobody might know who that is. It also goes some ways toward proving my point about what a pile of porcupine pellets that book is full of and how little those writers really know about so-called "Dog-Nose" Cooper.

The book I am talking about is of course the one that

just came out to such great hoo-ha and is called *Guide: The Life of W.C. Cooper—A Legend in His Own Time*, which is about as overblown a title as the man himself was. So it fits.

What gets my goat is how come those so-called writers never did come to ask me anything about old Dog-Nose while they were writing the book? They say themselves right on page 63 about how I was his partner for ten years and right up to the time of his disappearance. They always write the "mysterious" disappearance though I know exactly what happened to him. And it seems to me that if somebody saw what happened to somebody, then it ain't mysterious. It sure as hell was peculiar, but it wasn't mysterious. But they never came to ask me anything, and I just want to say that if they had, the book would not be so full of misinformation and nonsense and "mysterious" disappearances. I have a funny feeling that somebody must have tipped those writers off about how I didn't have anything too good to say about Dog-Nose and might kind of put a tarnish on the legend they were trying to embellish.

Anyway, I feel that if a man has got information that can clear up errors and misinformation, he has got a duty to bring those facts to the light. And that is why I am writing this piece. Like those writers said on page 63, I was Dog-Nose's partner in our guiding business (but for twelve years and not ten) and I was with him at the end. You could check on this by asking around, but as I said, most would know me as Junior and not as Ishmael.

One thing is that Dog-Nose is dead and not run off with

the half-dozen assorted wives and daughters that so many men have claimed and is still alive and living off in Idaho or some-place. Not true. He is dead and I saw him die and I don't know where all those women ran off to but it was not with Dog-Nose Cooper. I have seen that sort of thing happen before where a man makes out how his wife ran off with some "Legend" or other just to save face from having to admit she ran off because he was impossible to live with and in fact there was not any other man at all. So take my sworn word on it. Dog-Nose is long dead and did not run off with any woman.

That is not to say that he was not, at times, sorely in need of a woman as we both often were. There were stretches when I slept with four foot of pine limb under my bunk for fending off his occasional advances. I will not make out he was habitual at that kind of thing, but I will say he carried some pretty fair knots on his skull till the day he died. But that ain't one of the things I was planning on telling.

Before I get to the matter of his death, I would like to clear up that business of how he came to get that name Dog-Nose. You should understand that although we were partners in our guiding business, the proposition was not what you would call 50-50. What with his being the way he was, which was tall and of powerful build, and with his swelled head and educated speech and big mouth and easy-going manner with the sports, he got to handle the so-called public relations, and did the guiding, and played the role, and became the Legend. And I, being short and a little shy, and not real good at talking with much razzle-dazzle, got to do the cooking, and carrying the loads, and remaining relatively obscure. But we needed each other; he needing somebody to boss around and do the cooking, and I needing him as the drawing card, which he did real well, and we did split the take down the middle.

Anyway, about his getting the name Dog-Nose. What it says in the book is true as far as it goes. It is true we were guiding for Mr. John D. Tudrow, the New York millionaire, who came up to get bear. And it is true that Dog-Nose dropped to his knees on the trail real sudden with his nose to the ground and stayed like that for a spell and then says, "A bear has been here quite recently," is how he talked. And it is also true that right over the next rise was a trophy black bear that Mr. John D. Tudrow made short work of and then told just about everybody in the world how his guide, W.C. Cooper, had a nose as good as a dog's and could smell where game had passed. Well ever since that time, the name Dog-Nose has stuck, which is what everybody started calling him. And though it does not seem too flattering a name, he was glad to get it on account of up to that time everybody called him "Outhouse" because his initials were W.C. Naturally, the book does not tell you that.

What the book also does not tell is what all that supposed track-sniffing was really about. What happened was that we were walking along in our usual order with Dog-Nose out front like some kind of Great White Banana on a safari in Africa or something, and then the sports, who in this case were Mr. John D. Tudrow and his friend Mr. Eli McKee, and then me in the rear, lugging supplies. Well, Dog-Nose gets it in his head to drop back and grouse at me about something or other and while we are walking together behind the sports, Mr. McKee lets go of a springy little sapling that he has just pushed by. A quick sidestep was all that was needed to get out of its way (which I did), but Dog-Nose was too busy acting like a bigshot and never saw it coming. The little tree sprang right back and caught him square in the balls, from which you can believe that he doubled up right quick and hit the ground in a three-point landing on his nose and both knees. Of course the sports never realized what had happened, but just looked back to find Dog-Nose on the ground with his nose in the dirt, making noises like he is sniffing out game while in fact he is gasping for breath and turning as blue as a kingfisher. You have got to hand it to him for quick thinking in the face of imminent humiliation, but I can tell you as sure as I now breathe and he does not, that that bear being just over the rise as he predicted was pure, dumb luck of the highest degree and nothing else. He could not smell where game was any better than he could tell by that method whether he needed a bath.

Now I had better get to clearing up how he died before I run out of paper. It was back about the winter of 1968-69 that the whole thing started, and if those writers said he disappeared about the spring of 1969, then that is about right. Except of course he did not disappear, which I already explained.

We were staying in our cabin up in the North Bay area of Moosehead Lake during a slack time between jobs. I had just woken up and was sitting on the edge of my bunk, putting on my boots so as to stoke up the stove. You would not want to try walking across that floor barefoot on account of the fact that you would more than likely get frozen in your tracks for literal. So I was sitting on the edge of my bunk, which was the bottom one, Dog-Nose always making sure to get the top one on account of heat rises and so it is always warmer up there. Except he never looked before he swang down off his bunk, and on that particular morning that I am recalling, he came down square on the back of my neck, sending us both sprawled out in a tangled mess on the floor, and the first thing I realize is how I am out of reach of my club. Well I could see right then that a nasty scene was in the development, when a knock came on the door.

Now knocks on our door were not exactly a boring daily occurrence up in that wilderness, and I believe it was just about the only thing that could have happened to change Dog-Nose's course from what was on his mind at the moment.

What stood at our door, out in the snow, when it was opened by Dog-Nose made us both jump back in fright and fall into a tangled mess again. Except this time it was not planned. Here was about four-and-a-half feet of dried, yellow crud in more or less the shape of a small human. "Mr. Cooper," says the lump with the voice of Jimmy Warner, who lives with his widowed mom on a wilderness farm they have down near the south end of the bay, "you had best come quick. Mom has gone crazy and I can't calm her down," or words to that effect. So we get dressed and all set off across the ice toward the Warner farm while Jimmy relates how they have been losing chickens on a regular basis for about a month and were going to call on Dog-Nose anyhow sooner or later to track and kill the varmint that has been doing in the poultry. But a day or so before, the widow Warner was out investigating a commotion up the henhouse and came back a changed person for the worse. He goes on to tell how ever since, his ma has been mixing up enormous batches of mustard sauce and making one holy mess of the house and is out of her head. It was that mustard sauce that covered his whole body and had dried and caked and made him look like a yellow lump.

Well some couple hours later we circumvented the unfrozen spring hole that comes out in front of the farm and we were greeted by a sight to make a grown man groan, which we did, except for Jimmy. There were chicken feathers and bloody spots all over the snow near the shore, and by the time we got up to the porch we were all crying like babies on account of the fumes of mustard that were emanating from the house. Inside was a plastered mess of yellow sauce at every turn, and at the kitchen table about ankle-deep in the stuff is the widow

Warner mixing up still another ten-gallon batch with a look on her face that left no doubt as to how she was rowing with but one oar.

Taking his usual charge of a situation, the first thing Dog-Nose did was cold-cock her with a mixing spoon and lay her out on the parlor sofa where there was not yet too much mustard sauce plastered about. Then he orders me to fix a batch of sassafras tea while he goes out to have a look around. While he is out being a legendary guide and tracker and what-not, the widow comes around and I and Jimmy give her a cup of the sassafras tea to calm her poor mind, and she quiets down some but still has the faraway look in her eyes and does not know me from atoms, nor her own son neither.

Well the "Legend" comes back in his own time, and has got a look on his face like he has taken in all there is to be seen and is now ready to let it set and stew and mull for a spell. So we break open a bottle of the widow's best Scotch and bide our time while she lays there mumbling incoherently, and Jimmy sets out to scraping the mustard sauce off the walls and floors, and Dog-Nose gets to thinking out loud:

"It is a curious thing," says Dog-Nose, "how there are only feathers of the Barred Plymouth Rocks out on the snow. Yet those I have observed in the henhouse roost farthest from the door. The Rhode Island Reds roost closest to the door, but they have not been touched. Isn't that right, Jimmy?"

"Yep," says Jimmy, breaking out of his crust finally. "We

had twelve Plymouth Rocks and now we has three, and the Reds ain't been touched."

"Well I, for one," says Dog-Nose, "am not familiar with any predator that exhibits such an extreme of selectivity. I am truly at sixes and sevens," and falls down dead drunk.

Next morning, we are awakened by the widow Warner mixing up another furious batch of mustard sauce and this time I cold-cock her myself with the empty Scotch bottle. Just then Jimmy comes running in with the news that another hen has been taken and that there are fresh tracks in the new snow that fell while we were asleep. Well, he did not need to say any more before Dog-Nose is outside with his little bags of plaster of Paris making casts of every little mark on that fresh snow, half of which were his own tracks but saying he could not be too careful.

We were at the Warner farm for most of two months trying to figure out what it was taking the chickens, which had stopped being bothered pretty much what with one or another of us sleeping out in the henhouse every night and trying to keep the widow from filling the house with mustard sauce. Dog-Nose spent most of each day staring at those plaster casts he had made, and every so often looked like he had come on to something but would never say. One time I found him in a kind of daze like he had seen Jesus or somebody. And another time I caught him in the kitchen, all het up, mixing up just a little cup of mustard sauce. But mainly he just stared at those casts and said nothing.

To me, those casts and the tracks and marks that they were made from did not appear like anything I could make heads nor tails out of nor feet neither. There were parts that looked like where something had been dragged along the snow, like a boat or sled maybe, but there were not any footprints of them who would have done the dragging. Then there were parts that looked like they were made by duck feet or something, but about the size of a Chevrolet. Plus, there were various other marks and prints that looked like a confusion of nothing much to me, but then I was no Legend.

Around the first week of April, Dog-Nose finally comes out of his funk and begins packing up his kit and says to me: "I am going back to the cabin to do a few things and to get some gear together. You are to remain here and look after the widow and the boy. Do not prevent her from making more mustard sauce if she wants to. I will return in ten days."

So for the next ten days, me and the boy took to filling every container of every size on that farm with the mustard sauce that the widow was producing in prodigious amounts. And on the fifteenth of April, back came Dog-Nose as promised with a glaze in his eye, a determined set to his jaw, and a pack full of whatall. We go into the kitchen and sit down at the table.

"Junior," he says to me real intensely, like he is posing for some big magazine interview that is doing an article about him titled 'The Greatest Guide in the Whole World Ever,' "I have solved the mystery. I know what took those chickens, and I am going to catch it."

And with that he unloads from his pack a hundred feet of quarter-inch nylon rope and what looks like a dead Barred Plymouth Rock chicken. After I pick it up, I realize that what it is is a gigantic trout fly that Dog-Nose has tied out of a half-dozen grizzly saddle-hackle patches and onto what looks to be about a size 50/0 tuna hook.

"There is a colossal trout out there, Junior," he says. And with that the widow goes into a frenzy of unparalleled mustard sauce production until Jimmy cold-cocks her with a shovel.

"Today is opening day, Junior," continues Dog-Nose, "and it is going to be the greatest day of my career so far."

And he proceeds to tie a Turle knot onto that giant fly with the rope and heads on down to the shore by the spring hole. He lays the coil of rope down by his feet and signals me to stand clear as he begins swinging that fly around and around over his head like a helicopter and lets it go. Out it shoots over the water with the rope coming off in loops from the coil, and it plunks down about fifty feet out and sinks. We watch that rope for any tugs or jerks, but it just stays still and finally goes slack when the fly hits bottom.

Then Dog-Nose starts pulling the fly back in with little yanks, letting the loops of rope fall around his feet, when all of a sudden the surface swells and that rope starts going back out again like a bolt of lightning. And those loops that Dog-Nose let drop by his feet start whipping and flying, and before we knew it they are wrapped around his legs and there he goes.

I only saw him alive once more and that was on the trout's first jump. There was still some pretty thick ice out on the lake, but that fish just came right up through it. It was like a silver mountain risen from the water, and there was the fly in its gigantic lip, looking about like a number 26 midge, and the rope ran on back over its gill cover, which looked to be about the size of a barn door. And there, all tangled in the rope, back below the dorsal fin and snug against the gleaming side, was old Dog-Nose, kicking and hollering to no avail. Then the fish fell back crashing through the ice like the end of the world.

After a spell she came up again, just kind of a roll, and I caught a quick glimpse of Dog-Nose still tangled secure against her side. He was quiet now, though, and was not fighting any more.

When she came up the third time it was like all hell broke loose. She stood on her tail and whipped her head, trying to shake that fly, and her shining body blocked out half the far shoreline, although she was a hundred yards out. And I saw Dog-Nose still tied on, limp and broken as a kid's doll, and I knew it was all over for him for sure. He and the trout went down for the third and last time, the waters closing over them calm and cold like it has been for the last thousands of years, little chickadees whistling on the shore and crows wheeling against the spring sky. The Legend-in-his-own-time had run out of time. And I have run out of paper.

2
BACK AGAIN

Well, you don't know what we can find,
Why don't you come with me, little girl,
On a magic carpet ride?

— Steppenwolf

Well, here I am back again. And I can tell you that there is nobody more surprised to see it than this old geezer who is writing this, yours truly. I have now become a full-blown writer as a direct result of the piece you just read as Chapter 1, which I wrote a while back as a magazine article called "For the Record." It was originally called "For the Record" on account of its being for the purpose of setting the record straight on the life and times of one W.C. "Dog-Nose" Cooper (who everybody and his uncle at least have heard about, mostly wrong), only now it has grown into a full-blown project of massive proportions that is to be hereafter known as *The Dog-Nose Chronicles* and that is to serve the very same purpose as the first piece only moreso.

But maybe you have been in a coma or someplace these past few years and do not know what I am talking about. It was all started by the coming out of a pissant book about Dog-Nose that was full of very bad misinformation and general pasture patties. In a fit of temporary loss of all good sense I took pen in hand, as they say, though it was actually a pencil at the time but that is an expression I have read some writers using, and I wrote the piece that you have read as Chapter 1, although you probably already read it in the magazine when it first came out. Well, aside from making me a quick buck or two and getting the gripe off my chest, I figured that was all there was to it. I was never so wrong about anything since the time I made up a batch of two dozen loaves of bread for the Cutler party (which we were guiding) with what I thought was flour but what turned out to be Dog-Nose's goddam store of plaster of Paris that he used for making casts of animal tracks.

Letters came pouring in almost from the week that piece came out. Most folks were all het up to be hearing more about myself and Dog-Nose and the time we spent together in our guiding business, which made me kind of start thinking I might give a whirl to an expanded project, what with writing seeming to come somewhat naturally to me as I found out from writing the original piece. But there were a few letters that came from some real hotheads. Those that wrote them had a couple of harsh words for yours truly about the stability of my mental faculties and the questionable state of my sobriety. They were all pretty sore about what one of them called my "jaundiced attempt to denigrate the reputation of one of America's greatest folk heroes." Well it was those kinds of remarks, few as they were compared to the overwhelming majority that expressed real interest, that made me think "Oh yeah? Well you have not heard anything yet if you want to see some reputations get denigrated, weasel face."

Imagine the ignorance of him who wrote such a thing, anyway. "One of America's greatest folk heroes," he says. Who does he think he is talking about? Paul Bunyan or Casey at the Bat or somebody? Dog-Nose Cooper was a real person, not some made-up figment. That is the whole trouble with those hotheads. They have lost their perspective about how he was a real person with real tendencies to being an asshole just like everybody. He was not some perfect "folk hero." And it was thinking on thoughts like that that made me think harder and harder about writing more and explaining things that needed telling.

But what really clinched the whole deal was a letter I got from a lady I never expected to hear from. In fact, I was not really sure she existed at all. Those idiots who wrote the other book have got her mentioned on page 48 for a couple lines, but what with all the other nonsense they have passed off as gospel, who could be sure? I can tell you, though, that after I got her letter I was all set to go and no stopping me. I went out and bought a stack of paper, a used typewriter that I finally learned to play after a week of catching my finger between the buttons, and a fat book that all good writers use as was told to me by the lady in the book store. It is called *Roget's Thesaurus*, and before she explained that it was a book that gives a writer lots of ten-dollar words for all his little nickel ones, I was convinced of its being a storybook about some French kid and his pet dinosaur.

Now before I get to explaining about the letter from the lady and what it was that made me go ahead with this whole book, I would like to say that the copy of the original piece that is called Chapter 1 of this book is a nearly exact copy of the piece as it appeared in the magazine and which caused all the hubbub. Even though I have had a good deal more practice at writing and recognize some places where I would like to make what we writers call stylistic changes, and even though my editors have taken a hand at correcting my grosser grammatical delinquencies throughout the rest of the book, I have insisted that the original piece be pretty much left alone. That way nobody can claim that I am trying to extenuate the so-called jaundice. So that's that.

Now for the letter. It was obviously from a female as I could tell right off from the penmanship, and it was a shock to say the least. It was peculiar enough to be getting a letter from a woman, what with every single piece of mail that I had gotten so far being from the males of the species, but I had just been sitting there thinking that very observation when the envelope came, and that was what was so shocking. But that was not anything to what was coming. Here is the letter.

5 Brattle Street
Cambridge, Mass.

January 19, 1983

Dear Junior,

I do not know if my late husband has ever mentioned me to you. We had not been living as husband and wife for many years before his death, fifteen at least, though we had never actually taken any action toward a formal divorce. You see, I still loved him very much, perhaps still do, and had always retained the hope that he would come back to me. When he left, it was not with a feeling of malice and finality, but with that inconclusive indifference with which he seemed to stumble upon all his decisions to act. You are no doubt familiar with that aspect of his character.

I say that because, having read your article entitled "For the Record," I was impressed by your attitude toward him. You seem to have, much the way I have, loved him very much. I doubt you could have remained close friends and business partners for so long other-wise. Yet you have apparently not been taken in by that peculiar gift of his which seems to have caused nearly the entire country to deify him to such an extraordinary degree. More importantly, however, you seem not particularly averse to making a target of yourself by putting in print what an utter shithead he could be at times.

That is why I have decided to make known to you, and to put at your disposal, some writings I have in my possession. Even Baker and

Gilroy are ignorant of the existence of these papers, for when they interviewed me as part of their research for that obsequious book of theirs, I was so taken aback by their sycophantic adulation of the "Legend" to whom I had been married, that I refused to give them even the slightest information about him or our life together. Needless to say, I now feel that my intuition might have been divinely guided.

The papers are part of a book he was writing. Naturally, the book was to be autobiographical, a memoir, more or less, though it was to include personal essays and natural history as well as narrative. He started it while we were still together, and he left it in my care when he left. For years thereafter, even when only a fool as myself would have failed to realize he was never coming back, he continued to send packages containing pages for the book. No letters ever accompanied the writings, not a word of personal correspondence. He seemed to know, with an understanding of me more complete than that which even I had of myself, that they would simply be taken care of. Even during your own years with him, he continued to write and send packages filled with text. You are probably not even aware of that. He could certainly be a secretive son of a bitch.

In any regard, I will gladly make those papers available to you if you wish to continue your promising writing career by producing an expanded work based upon your years with my husband. You would be free to include his writings verbatim, if you wished, and to provide any additional explanatory or qualifying comment that you saw fit. I would attach no strings.

I offer only this modest bit of advice. Avoid making more of the homosexuality to which you have made innuendoes in your original piece. It is seriously misleading and undoubtedly anomalous. Despite his enormous sexuality—the man was in a constant state of rut while we were together, and when I could not satisfy his nearly continual needs, he would take them elsewhere—he was, I am certain, strictly heterosexual. It was a rare woman in our neighborhood, young or old, who had not been bedded by the great "Legend." I can suggest only that the exigencies of your lives in the wilderness or, perhaps, a particularly muliebrous derriere on your part may have induced his uncharacteristic pederasty if, indeed, such goings-on truly occurred. But the man did have an appetite like a goat and a set of nuts the likes of which I have not seen again.

Do please let me know of your decision, Junior. I remain,

Mrs. W.C. Cooper

Now there was a gal with a copy of *Roget's Thesaurus*! It did not take but a few minutes to make the decision to write her back and okay the deal. And that is when I went out and bought all the trappings to go whole hog into the writing business. But as for my "muliebrous derriere" I will tell you this: a shaggier bum than mine I have never seen on any female but for a Lab bitch we owned named Gorilla. I will also say this: I never said in Chapter 1 that Dog-Nose did anything but make "occasional advances," and to be perfectly accurate, as is my intention throughout this book, I must admit that even those may have been largely imagined due to the "exigencies of your lives in the wilderness," as the lady so aptly put it. So that is the last I will say of it.

So after a while the papers came in by the United Parcel Service, and they filled a box that could have held a brace of full-grown Brittanies without cramping them any. I cannot say for certain whether it is regrettable or lucky for everyone involved, but in my opinion about ninety percent or better of the writings in that box were about as clear as Grand Lake Stream at ice-out, which if you were ever in Maine at that time of year you would know is about like mud itself.

Most were scientific writings of the most starchy kind, and though I knew Dog-Nose had been to college, I was not aware of the extent to which he had put his learning. He had written articles and papers on just about every animal and fish you were likely to meet. And from what I could gather from the Latin of things, a few pounds worth were devoted entirely to insects that live in the water. There is no question as to how he knew his mayflies and caddis and stones and midges and what-not when it came to matching hatches and advising sports, but again I had no idea of the scholarly extent of it. And if the value of those scientific papers is measured by boring writing and unreadable style, the man was a genius.

As I said, about better than ninety percent of the papers were of that sort, and if I were to include any of that in this book, I would end up with something that could put a man to sleep faster than a blow to the head from a low-hanging limb. It would be the kind of book where if a person had been suck-ing on tea bags and chewing coffee grounds all day and needed something that could put him to sleep real quick despite all that, he would just lay down with this book and read a page or two of Dog-Nose's articles. But that is not what I am after, and neither is it all of what Dog-Nose wrote either. The ten percent that is the good stuff is enough to give a reader a pretty fair feeling for the man who wrote it. And there is no arguing about the fact that all the biographying in the world is not worth a bucket of fish slime against the words set down by a man himself. So here is a piece from the writings of W.C. "Dog-Nose" Cooper that has not been edited nor touched-up by me and is just as it came from the box.

***

KILLS

At the edge of the stream, the horizontal bank is suddenly distorted by a great uplifting of roots. The oak that once stood beside the water had long ago fallen away from the stream and exposed its secret underside, creating a small embayment or backwater and a slight undercut below the mat of watercress. In the watercress, the insects of the stream take refuge, find food, mate, and die. The undercut backwater with its cover of watercress provides the trout that holds that spot with everything it needs. And the trout that holds it must be able to fend off continual challenges, for the spot is one of the best in the stream. By holding the spot for a season, a trout can thrive to the point of being almost certain to hold it yet another sea-son. And so the backwater beneath the upturned roots invariably embraces the largest brown trout in that part of the stream.

In the spring of the year, down among the stems of watercress in the green light that filtered down through the floating leaves, the nymphs of black-winged damselflies crawled. They had hatched from eggs laid last summer and spent the winter as nymphs in the stream's bottom. In the lengthening days of the new spring, the watercress grew, and the tiny nymphs crawled up into the plants and thrived on the abundance of other insects there. Some avoided the small trout that, before being eaten by the big brown below the roots, cruised the watercress for food. Some, too, escaped the jaws of the other myriad killers in the weeds: dragonfly nymphs, diving beetles, water bugs, crayfish. Those that survived grew, and when they were ready, they climbed the underwater stems of the watercress until their wiggling bodies broke through the surface into a new element. Then they waited in the sun for their old skins to split open and let their new bodies out.

The landing net, attached to the spring-loaded cable clipped to the back of his fishing vest and tucked into the large back pocket was caught by a twig of streamside clethra as he moved through the woods. The twig lifted the net from the pocket of the vest and drew the cable out of the retractor. By the time he felt the tug that signaled the extent of the cable's length, the twig released its grasp on the net. The spring in the retractor performed its job admirably, and the net was yanked back by the cable until the butt struck him at the base of his skull. He shook off the familiar pain and took the few remaining steps to the stream's edge. The water was now settled to its early-summer depth, still deep and forceful but with a contentment as different from the spring rush and chaos as the scattered, leisurely damselflies now were from the swarming, urgent mayflies of weeks past.

He stood on the bank, knee deep in sensitive ferns and grasses, shaded by a swamp maple with several trunks, one of which bent low and far out over the stream. The sweeper spread just thirty feet down-stream from the spot beneath the roots of the dead oak. On the far bank, wild grapes piled their vines upon each other and overhung the water. Yellow warblers nested in them by the golden dozens and flashed back and forth across the stream all spring and summer calling "see-see-see-titi-wee." He rested the butt of his rod in the branches of a shrub and strung the line from the reel up through the guides. He straightened the coiled leader with his fingers as the heat from the friction and the pulling relaxed the nylon. Then he paused and watched the stream.

Out of its split nymphal skin, hugging an emergent shoot of watercress, squeezed a slender metallic abdomen, neon green. The damselfly arched and then straightened its body and began working on freeing its four velvet-black wings. The old skin split further, expos-ing the black bundle on its back. The male black-winged damselfly sat very still as its wings expanded, straightened, and dried.

Farther upstream, a female black-winged damselfly, duller than the male, its wings less brilliantly black but graced with a spot of white on each, had emerged two hours earlier than the downstream male. Her charcoal wings now stretched straight and slender over her abdomen as she perched on an oak twig in a little clearing in the woods. Sunlight filtered down through a hole in the leafy canopy and spotlighted the patch of air she was watching. Glinting speckles of floating dust rose from the dry leaves on the ground and drifted in the shaft of light, falling, rising again, shifting slightly but suddenly to the left and right in tiny invisible downdrafts and eddies of warming air. Suddenly, a midge, tiny but boldly highlighted in the sunray, crossed the little clearing, and the female damselfly darted out and gathered it into the basket formed of her legs. Then she returned to her perch and ate it, watching for another.

31

A quiet rise caught his attention as he stood on the bank watching the stream. The rings were upstream of the maple sweeper, just out from the grapevines opposite the uprooted oak. He would have to enter the stream above the sweeper and stay just about there. He could not tell what the trout had risen to, but he suspected it was an ant. Ants often fell off another large maple sweeper farther upstream, and he had always had good results with ants on this stream at this time of year. He opened the zippered pocket of his vest that contained the box of terrestrials and picked from the box a small, black ant of black Poly and white wings made of feather tips. He always made his ants with wings because he could not see them otherwise. The white wings showed up against the dark water like little flags of surrender. He tied the ant onto his tippet and dipped it in a bottle of floatant. Then he waited a minute or two while it dried.

The male black-winged damselfly sat upon the emergent shoot of watercress and dried its newly expanded wings. They were so black and new they showed no detail, just blackness. He gave them a few exploratory flutters. They responded, and with the peculiar motion of black-winged damselflies, the motion of petals falling or a small round of quiet applause, the male rose from its shoot and flew a few feet to a new perch on a twig of viburnum. There it rested.

He climbed cautiously down the bank and entered the stream just above the sweeper. The water came right to his waist. He eased out, walking sideways like a crab, his back to the sweeper, and felt the push of the stream against his legs. His right foot hit against a rock on the stream bottom, and he almost fell. He moved around it and took a few shuffling strides upstream, nearly tripping over another rock. The trout rose again, just beneath the grapes this time but in the same general spot. Because of the sweeper close behind him, no backcast was possible. He finally accepted that fact after uncountable past

*attempts at launching the backcast above the sweeper. Now failure
was even more certain, for over the years, new growth on the topside
of the sweeper had grown tall. In the past, a backcast over the
sweeper may have been possible with greater skill than he pos-
sessed. Now it was impossible. But the sweeper had taught him to be
a fairly expert roll-caster.*

*He rolled out a cast that fell a few feet short of the last rise, and
he let the line drift back a ways without taking any in and rolled out
another cast. That one dropped the ant nicely above the last rise and
in the proper line of drift. His pleasure bordered on surprise, but he
decided that his skill was improving and that casts like that should be
expected of him from now on. He stripped in line as the fly drifted
toward him and over the lie of the trout. As he prepared for another
cast, the trout rose again, though not to his ant, and he felt relieved
that he had not put the trout down.*

As he flew farther upstream, from viburnum perch to sassafras
to oak to azalea, the new male was met by other males displaying
their displeasure with his invasion of their territories. Driven farther
from the stream, he alit on a maple twig in a little clearing in which the
sun poured through a break in the canopy and lit the quiet, drifting
dust particles that rose from the dry litter on the forest floor. There he
was beaten to a meal of midge by a female who, upon finishing her
meal, fluttered off toward the stream. The male followed.

*He rolled out another cast. The ant hit the edge of the
grapevines but, after panic briefly gripped his chest, fell off onto the
water. It drifted six inches and disappeared in a snapping rise. He
was never prepared for a take. After years of fishing and thousands
of strikes, he was still amazed when his fly disappeared. To him, a
trout taking an artificial fly, especially one he had tied himself, was
a miracle more splendid than birth. And more miraculous yet was
that after he overcame his surprise at the strike and stripped in his*

slack line and raised his rod tip, the trout was hooked. It dashed out toward midstream and leapt, lustrous, into the air.

The female damselfly reached the edge of the stream and perched upon the upturned root of a huge, fallen oak. The male, close behind, hovered before her, beating his delicate, inky wings faster and faster. The female responded with a dance of her own, and the male landed on her back as she perched upon the oaken root above the weedy backwater. There they mated, their abdomens linked and looped and clasped to each other.

His rainbow trout gave him a good run. It was not a large trout in the grand scheme of things, but for that stream it was noteworthy. It made several thrilling jumps that splashed water high in the grapevines. It dashed back and forth across the stream while he fought to keep it from tangling in the weeds along the left bank. There was a point in the fight when the trout nearly succeeded in tangling itself in the watercress stems and breaking free, but he worked it away from the danger. The trout even once rushed straight at him, and he had to strip line in as fast as he was able in order to keep tension on the trout. Eventually he worked the trout toward him in ever decreasing arcs of struggle as the trout's energy spent itself on fruitless leaps and bursts upstream. Then he led the trout into his tattered net and grasped it firmly in his shaking hand as he unhooked it and untangled it from the ravelled, cotton strands.

He held the shining rainbow trout and felt it flexing in his grip, its strength still impressive after its exhausting struggle. He nearly always released the trout he caught but decided to keep this one. It was the perfect size for a meal, and it was firm and solid and beautiful. It always bothered him to kill a trout, even to eat, but he held back his aversion to the task, gripped the trout tightly around its middle, and snapped his arm sharply down so that the trout's head cracked solidly against the handle of his net. The trout shuddered once and lay limp,

and he felt its life drain away, or at least he thought he did. Whether
real or imagined it saddened him, and he quickly slid the dead fish
into his creel.

When their mating upon the upturned oak root was done, the
black-winged damselflies untied themselves from each other and fluttered to the water like falling maple keys. The male perched upon a
fern frond that overhung the water, and from there he watched for the
approach of intruding males while his mate alit upon an emergent
shoot of watercress below.

He unhooked his ant from the net, reeled in the slack line,
hooked the ant to the keeper above his rod grip, and reeled the line a
little tighter to secure the ant. Then he worked his way upstream a few
dozen yards, passing the great upturned roots of the fallen oak where
black-winged damselflies fluttered above the mat of watercress in
which he nearly lost his trout. Stubbing his boot on a submerged and
ancient root, he swamped his chest waders as his balance failed him
and his feet could find no purchase on the slippery rocks below. The
surprising shock of cold water caused a gasp that deeply sucked the
stream into his lungs, and he thrashed and clawed in panicked horror
at the realization that this had finally happened.

The female damselfly backed slowly down the watercress stem
until her abdomen and ovipositor entered the water. As the male stood
guard above, she released a small batch of eggs on the plant stem
beneath the water and crawled back up. Then she fluttered a foot
downstream toward the edge of the weed bed and backed slowly
down another stem. As the tip of her abdomen pierced the surface of
the water, a large brown trout, perhaps the largest in the stream, rose
quietly from its lie in the undercut backwater beneath the upturned
roots and sipped her in without a sound. Only a perfect ring of distur-
bance on the stream's slick surface marked her passing, and that only
for a brief moment as it elongated, distorted, slid downstream, and

spread into liquid sameness with the run. The male damselfly, finding himself alone after a while, wandered off along the flowing water. He briefly investigated a floating form, sliding downstream as well, struggling briefly, twitching like a large damaged fish, then lying still, caught by the maple sweeper as the water piled up gently against my father's lifeless face.

Then the black-winged damselfly fluttered off into the woods to begin his pursuit of a new mate. A yellow warbler sang "see-see-see-titi-wee," and the stream breathed its eternal narrative to the woods.

3
STARTING OUT

When I think back
On all the crap I learned in high school
It's a wonder
I can think at all

— Paul Simon

Well, I guess it is about time I got around to explaining how it all got started. It is what I reckon might be called unorthodox by some to have started this book with what seems to be the end of itself, but that is merely because of that magazine article, now Chapter 1, not being expected to go any further, as I explained in the last chapter. If I had planned to make a book in the first place, you can bet I would have saved the end for the end. But that is not how things work out sometimes, and I will have to think of a different end for the end when I get there. That is not for you to worry about, though, for you can bet your last genuine junglecock neck that I will come up with something as I always do in a pinch. Anyway, there are plenty of good books that are considered famous and literate that start at the end and go backwards from there. I have read that it is an accepted literary technique even though I cannot right now tell you the names of any books that use it. But if I think of any later I will let you know. The only differ-ence is that those books were usually planned that way.

Anyway, as I was saying, it is about time I got to telling how I and Dog-Nose met up and started our guiding business together and how he became the Legend somewhere down the line. Actually there is probably some exact point when you could put your finger on it and say "That is the point when he became the Legend" on account of some event either real or exaggerated and advertised to the hilt by me in an effort to drum up business. And what I am trying to say here without too much of what you might call your self-incrimination is that I am as much responsible and to blame for this whole Legend business as anybody. But that is a part of this story that comes later along the line, and I have already jumped ahead of my story before I even started it.

Myself, I am originally Canadian. That may come as some shock to those who have thought I am American on account of how I sound in my writing, but it is not so. I am from Canada and was born in the province of Nova Scotia, which is sticking out over Maine quite a ways, for those who do not know the geography of the place too well. If I feel like it later, I will tell more about my growing up and personal stories from my own childhood, but right now it is how I met Dog-Nose that is important, and I had best get right to it.

Dog-Nose of course was American, and I met him for the first time one spring when he came up to Nova Scotia for some salmon fishing. We were both the same age, which was late twenties as I recall it, but in any other way you can think of, we were as different as a sucker and a grilse. He was in graduate school at the time or just out of it. I have forgotten which. And I was running my own bakery in town on most days and doing a little local guiding on the river for sports who came up from the States on weekends. But that is not to say that I did not do plenty of fishing on the river on those days when I should have been working the bakery and had no sports to guide, either. In fact, I was not doing so well in the bakery that I did not have to supplement my earnings with the occasional salmon to feed me in times of a shortage of bread, as it were. I guess you can see how it was a kind of vicious cycle, because if I had worked the bakery instead of fishing, I would not need the salmon to feed myself and on and on. But that is the way it was.

You must understand the setup on the particular pool I am going to be talking about here. There is a road along the south side of the river and one along the north side. But the one along the north side is back aways from the river and you have to drive up a kind of dirt road to a little parking area and then walk down a path through the shrubbery until you come out on the bank above the pool. That is the place where most of the local fellows come when they are going to fish that pool, and they sit on a little bench aways up on the bank and wait their turn. Those who do not know any better, like sports from the States who have not hired a guide, or even some of the locals who have no consideration for the unwritten rules of the place, just park on the other road. That road, the one on the south side of the pool, is right along the bank and you can park there and climb right down to the pool from the road.

Working the pool from both sides at once is not real pleasant. For one thing it makes you think you are on one of those crowded streams in the States where everybody is standing shoulder to shoulder like on a subway. That kind of thing was not necessary on that river, especially back in those days, and it still is not even like that today unless you make it like that by being inconsiderate and pushy. For another thing it is not all that great for the fishing when the jerks on the south side practically wade right out into the best parts of the pool and spook the hell out of every damn salmon in it.

Anyway, that is just how I and Dog-Nose met, what with me fishing from the north side like I was supposed to do and him clomping down the south bank from his Jeep and wading right out into the damn pool across from me as though I did not exist or had no business being there or did not matter one way or another.

The pool is about ninety feet wide, depending on the level of the water, and about the length of a football field. So a person has usually got his line out and working the pool anywhere from about twenty feet out to maybe two-thirds of the way across. When some fool is working the pool from the south side like he is not supposed to and he is not being particularly careful about not interfering with the person who is working it from the north side like it is supposed to be worked, you can see how there might be the occasional overlapping of lines around mid-pool. But I have to admit that even though he was working the pool from the wrong side and making me geared up for a fight in the doing of it, Dog-Nose was being careful enough about not interfering with my working the pool as I wanted to, and he was fishing pretty well downstream so as not to challenge my right to most of the pool.

We were both fishing wet flies, and I was getting less and less het up as I saw how he was not really spoiling anything by his presence, when I suddenly saw a great boil under my fly, and all the boys setting up on the bench let out some hoots and wows and could see from that vantage point that a big silvery salmon has risen up for my fly but has not taken it. And the commotion did not escape the attention of that young fellow across the pool neither. Well, I laid a couple more casts with that fly over the hole where that fish was laying but to no avail, as I had suspected. So I bring in my line and change to a big fluffy dry fly that I know will bring him out again. Meanwhile, that fellow across the pool starts in casting over my fish with his wet, and I can hear the whispered grumblings up on the bench behind me, and I know they are all shocked to see the balls on this stranger who is actually casting to a fish somebody else has raised and is still fishing for. I could not believe it myself. It called for some retaliation and no mistaking it, but I was not so hot-headed as to seek my revenge and queer the pool while there was still an interested fish to be raised. First things first after all, and the stranger was not having any success with that wet fly anyhow.

So I get my big fluffy white MacIntosh dry fly tied on and soaked with floatant and am whipping it back and forth to dry it when I see the stranger squinting over my way and then looking in his fly box. And I see him extract something big and white and fluffy that looks just like the MacIntosh I have just tied on myself, and he brings in his own line real quick and bites off the wet and starts tying on the dry. Well I sure as hell knew what was afoot then and take my good time and send out a fine cast of about forty-five feet that sets that fly down at the edge of that hole like a puff of milkweed seed, and she drifts down across that black patch and up rises this black and silver nose with an open mouth underneath, just ready to suck her in, when the goddamn fly starts to drag. And the nose drops back down under water. The gasps and aaawwws from the bench were enough to remind you of a great tree blowing and groaning in the wind, and it was apparent to me right away that my angle of attack on this fish was okay for a wet fly but too sharp downstream for a dry. So I start crabwise downstream so I can cast more straight across and not have to worry about the line getting pulled out straight at the last second again. My heart and adrenalin are pounding around so hard I have forgotten about the stranger altogether, and I get to my new position and start laying out another good cast. And as my white fluffy fly drops down just exactly were I want it, suddenly it turns into two white fluffy flies that go drifting down across that hole like two guys riding motorcycles next to each other down the middle of the highway.

Well now I say to myself: "Should I hook that weasel's line and teach him a lesson about how we do things around here, or should I work on that fish and the hell with him?" Naturally I decide in favor of the fish and simply lift up my fly at the end of its drift and lay it back down again at the top of the hole. And there are two of them again, floating like twins about one inch apart, and up comes that shiny nose again with the big open mouth and the two flies drift right in.

Down goes the nose. I look real quick across the pool and I see that fellow grinning at me like some fool 'possum, and I realize that I am doing the same back at him and am not the least bit mad. Then we both lift our rods and, bingo! Both of us have got that salmon hooked good and solid in both corners of its mouth from opposite sides of the river. I have never heard any kind of noise like what was coming from the bench neither before nor since. And I have never had any experience that would have taught me what to do in any case like that nor how the hell to play partnership fishing. So I back up onto the dry gravel to get some footing for when that fish finally gets wise and goes berserk and tangles those lines into some kind of Bimini Twist, but nothing happens. That fish just lays there with a hook on each side of its face, not seeing any advantage to going one way or the other. And I am thinking how if that salmon had anything to work with besides that pea-size brain, he would make short work of weaving himself a hammock out of our lines out there in mid-river and take it easy until such time as he decides to go nuts and tear hell out of about $500 worth of combined tackle. But the damn thing is just laying there doing nothing and I and the stranger are still grinning at each other and holding onto our rods like we were in some public toilet somewhere and just waited for the explosion.

After about a minute of this we were getting used to the fact that we have got a fish on our hands that has gotten himself confused into absolute immobility, and there is nothing going to happen unless we make a move. And I see the stranger starting to lean back on his rod and apply some pressure, and I start to do the same. And just as our rods are bent about double, I hear the stranger yell: "Hey, friend, make a wish!" And I am caught up in the craziness of it all and know just what he means and do not give a damn neither. And we both lean back even farther on those rods until I hear a sound that calls to mind a 20-gauge shotgun going off somewhere close by. I look across the pool just in time to see what looks like a slow motion movie of tiny sparkling black slivers of graphite flying off in all directions, accompanied by limp fly line and flashing drops of exploding water and fish.

Everything happened at once. The stranger's leader snapped, his rod exploded into smithereens, and the fish finally decided to make his move. But I won the wish. I was still connected to 30 pounds of screaming meemies and was being taken for the kind of ride that gave me only one quick chance to notice the stranger, standing thigh-deep in the pool with the smoking shattered butt of his rod in one hand and the other hand on his belly, as he roared with the fullest, deepest laughter I had ever heard. And by the time I landed that beauty about a half-hour later and conked her on the head with a rock, here is the whole crowd from the bench down hooting and yelling and amongst them is that stranger who slaps me on the back and hands me an ice-cold beer and says things laughing and playing in such a way that makes me realize real clearly just how little I am mad at him and how much friendship I have for the fellow in some kind of true brotherhood that cannot be explained. Sure he is an obvious asshole, but there is also something about him that makes you feel like the two of you have been in an exclusive club together for a long time. Those last are not really my own words but are paraphrased from a well-educated sport we once guided for a week in Nova Scotia some years later. It is about how everybody felt who ever met Dog-Nose.

For some reason, although I am not the type who makes friends real quickly, he took to me like a brother, and I spent the next couple of weeks guiding him around the river and getting him into some good fish without him having to piss off anybody. In fact, the very folks who were most aghast by his original behavior were quickest to taking to him like one of our own. Within a couple days he was being invited right to the dinner tables of those who first could not believe what a shithead he was. And that is how things were with him for as long as I ever knew him from then on.

There was no denying that underneath all the bluster and brag and bullshit, which made up about seventy-five percent of Dog-Nose Cooper, was some solid know-how when it came to book learning about the outdoors. The man knew his flies and bugs and birds and animals and plenty about fishing and hunting in theory and some practice as well, and it was that twenty-five percent of very impressive savvy that made me think we could give a go to some kind of partnership in a guiding business as he had suggested after we had known each other for a time. And it was the bluster and brag and bullshit, in combination with that winning way he had and his good looks and education and fancy upbringing, that made me realize that this fellow was a walking and living and breathing advertising campaign and public relations goldmine all by himself. Of course I will not pretend to be so much a promotions genius as to say I could have foreseen the making of the Legend, but I did see his potential as a perfect drawing card, as I think I might have said once already before somewhere.

What he definitely did not have too much of was a good working understanding of things in the outdoors that we locals had been brought up with and took to be just common knowledge. He did not even know simple things like, for instance, that a gull flying inland meant rain to be coming. He laughed when I said it, but after I told him that my grandpappy, who was a fisherman all his life, had taught me that and much more such signs, and that it did indeed rain soon after I point-ed out to him all the gulls headed upcountry, he could not help but admit that there might be something to it. Better than that, though, was how we was fishing a pool one afternoon when some more gulls were headed inland, flying fairly low up the river, and one of them let go a load and missed Dog-Nose by about six inches. By the way, you should realized that at that time he did not yet have the name Dog-Nose, which he was to acquire sometime later in an incident that I described already in Chapter 1. He was called Outhouse up to that time, as I said, on account of his initials being W.C., which actually stood for Westlake Coleridge Cooper. But except for women who called him Wes, every man he knew called him Outhouse until he got the name Dog-Nose. But I am going to call him Dog-Nose even when I tell of times before he got that name because it is easier to keep things straight that way and because of this being called "The Dog-Nose Chronicles," which I otherwise would have to call "The Outhouse and Then The Dog-Nose Chronicles" if I were to follow any other method. So that is that.

As I was saying, this load of gull droppings comes falling out of the sky and splats in the river about six inches in front of Dog-Nose. And he yells over to me like it is the greatest thing that ever happened to him. "Hey, Junior, I just got missed by a load of gull flop."

"Well obviously you ain't familiar with the luck that can come from one of them things actually hitting you," I shout back dead serious, and he laughs some more. Sure enough, within about thirty seconds, a great boil comes under his fly but the salmon misses by just about six inches.

The next day we are fishing another pool upriver and the gulls start coming over again. All of a sudden I hear a mess of swearing and yelling from Dog-Nose and he says to me: "Hey, Junior, today must be my lucky day because I just got crapped on by another gull, fair and square." And I look over at him and sure enough he has one of those fine long streaks of whitewash blazed right down the front of his vest, which he is trying to splash with water to wash off the mess, and within thirty seconds he is hooked solid to a twenty-pounder that has come up under his fly and gobbled it in without him even noticing.

By the time he died, Dog-Nose believed a lot of things that he had at first laughed at when I told them to him, and he understood the outdoors a lot better on account of my teaching. It is true that he taught me a great deal as well, particularly concerning things that had to have been learned from books, like studies that had been done and life histories that could never be actually watched unless you had nothing else to do for the rest of your life but to follow this one insect or plant or animal around like the people who wrote the books. And he also had a good feeling for how those things all fit together and hung on each other. But he was pathetic on simple everyday things like knowing that a turtle always walks into the wind, or that woollybear caterpillars can tell how cold the winter will be, or that the doors of beaver lodges always face south, or that the age of a speckled trout is told by counting the number of spots that touch the base of its tail. There were plenty of things like that that he had no knowledge of whatever, and it was the learning of those kinds of things that eventually made him a better guide and person in the long run.

Anyway, on account of my being Canadian from Nova Scotia and Dog-Nose being American from New England, between us we had license to guide in a pretty fair spread of territory, which gave us a real nice benefit to prospective sports. That, plus my new-found talent for promoting whatever we had going for us, proved to be all we needed to get real well known real quick, as you will see. But I want to say right now that if it gets to sounding as though I am blowing my own horn too much about the smart ways we came up with for getting well known, that is not my intention. I am just telling how it was. Those are the facts, and that is all there is to that. Even if all my ideas never worked a bit and nobody ever knew us from atoms, I would still tell the same stories just the way they came out. In fact, there indeed were some times when things were not going so well and business was slow and we took to making a buck here and there in some pretty peculiar ways that do not fit too well with the whole Legend picture, if you know what I mean. Mainly there was a stretch in the early days when we were dealing with a fellow by the name of Sonny Lematina who is dead now, so I can write about him without worrying about getting sued. It all started with his chain of fur coat stores, which I recall as being called Clothes Encounters of the Furred Kind. And me and Dog-Nose were supposed to supply him with pelts, which we did in our own way until word got around about it and fouled him up and he took to smuggling drugs and getting arrested. But that is a whole other story and I will tell it later.

For now, I have found a poem in the box that Dog-Nose wrote back in the early days, and I thought it would make a good end to this chapter. I do not know for certain if it is a good one or not, but I like it, and it fits just fine with the subject that I have been writing about. So here it is just the way Dog-Nose wrote it:

SALMON RIVER

The lucky ones will run it,
    Down and back.
They are being readied for it,
    In their natal waters.
Branded with the taste and essence,
    Of this flowing track.
Children of the liquid silver,
    Speckled sons and daughters.

From the spawning lake they spill,
    Through the urgent runs.
Swept above the worried stones and grasses,
    Worn like old shawls.
Resting, watchful, in peat-stained pools,
    Ever the hunted ones.
They run the gantlet to the salt.
    The finish ribbon calls.

The lucky ones will make it,
    Birth to birth.
Their journey will return the flow,
    From end to source.
The song is a familiar one,
    Throughout the throbbing Earth.
Born to chase the river home:
    Parr for the course.

4
THE EARLY YEARS

No one will be watching us,
Why don't we do it in the road?

— The Beatles

Back when I and Dog-Nose first got started in the guiding business partnership, things were a little of what you might call lean. I am not talking now about those days when I was still running the bakery and guiding sports on the side, nor when Dog- Nose and I would take sports out on summer four-day holiday trips and the like while still having our hands in our own individual ways of making a buck for security. No, those days were fine, for we never lacked for sports to guide nor money in our pockets as I can recall.

It was not until we actually made the stick-out-your-neck commitment to the business by cutting loose every other form of safe income-earning opportunities that things got to where we were wondering what in hell we had gotten ourselves into and how come business suddenly dried up like a squashed frog on the summer tarmac. I have seen this kind of thing happen before, though in far less life-threatening ways, where you kind of feel out the situation little by little, cautious as can be, and then just when you reckon all is well and make the big step, everything goes wrong. It is like testing out the bottom of a new stream. You step real lightly and carefully off the bank, maybe still holding on to a branch or something. Then you ease out a little, moving your feet in tiny little shuffley steps. The bottom is nice and solid, no quicksand, no holes, and you finally let go of the branch and make your commitment and take your next step into some bottomless muck-hole that sucks you down and fills your waders.

That is how it seemed when we went full steam into our guiding business. It was just bad coincidence, not having anything to do with any changes we were making in the ways we handled things, but nearly as soon as we went full-time, all those steady customers got involved in other pursuits and we were handed nothing but a box full of time.

But it was not long before opportunity came knocking on our door, although that is only a figure of speech, for we actually saw him drive up in a late-model coupe and blow his horn in our yard. Here was one Sonny Lematina, a fellow of about our own ages who had come all the way up there just to find Dog-Nose and offer us a money-making proposition at a time when money-making propositions were not jumping out from behind every bush at us.

But first let me tell you about this Lematina character. He was a short, stocky fellow of about two hundred pounds. Then he took off the enormous raccoon coat he was wearing and proved himself to be a little puny runt of about one hundred-twenty pounds. But he was the big-city type that talked like a man with a lot more weight to throw around than what this squirt was carrying on his skinny bones. I had never seen much of this hatchet-faced type before, but there was a manner about him that gave me the feeling that I was dealing with some kind of quick and dangerous reptile full of teeth that would not only bite the hand that fed it but prefer the hand to the food.

He turns out to be an old acquaintance of Dog-Nose from high school. I say acquaintance because I could see right off from the way Dog-Nose is handling his greetings and conversation that this Lematina fellow was not ever Dog-Nose's close friend nor far friend neither. Dog-Nose is doing with his talk and his eyes just the kind of egg-walking that a person would do with his feet and body when coming suddenly face to face with an unexpected bear on a trail through the alders. There is a cautious and gentle side-stepping, backing, working around, and watching the eyes that gives an observer like myself no mistake about how Dog-Nose trusts this guy about like he trusts a cornered water snake.

But the guy's proposition seems straightforward enough, as far as it goes. He simply wants us to supply him with furs for his chain of fur-coat stores in New York, which he has called Clothes Encounters of the Furred Kind. It is apparently the terms of payment that Dog-Nose has some doubts about, but we were not in any kind of position to let any terms of payment go by at all. So Dog-Nose agrees to set up a series of traplines and see how things come out, and I notice that after we conclude our business there is not the customary invitation to dinner from Dog-Nose. So I follow his lead and do not open my big mouth, and Lematina gets back in his car and drives off, to where we do not know nor care.

As I had suspected, Dog-Nose does not, nor never has, liked the fellow. He tells me that they were in high school together and what a general pest and slimy character this Lematina was.

"He's the kind of person who, had I invited him to stay for dinner, would have somehow managed to relieve us of one leg from each of our chairs," Dog-Nose says. And he goes into the house to check our belongings even though Lematina had stood out in the yard with us the whole time.

"I will say this, though," said Dog-Nose, returning, "there is some money to be made here, assuming we ever get paid, and if we're as smart as we think we are, it ought not be too much work in the making of it."

"Well, first of all, " I say, "I ain't thought we was all that smart for the past few weeks anyway. But apart from that, I have run traplines before," say I, "and I can tell you that if you think we are about to fall into some easy money by that method, you have got a few miserable weeks coming. If we are to make the kind of money you have on your mind, we have got to run lines from here to Siberia. And short of that we are about to work our skinny asses to the bone anyway, trekking over chip and dale, setting and checking miles and miles of trapline in cold and snowy and wet weather and no guarantee that it all pays off either in skins nor your weasely friend's money in any case."

"You're wrong, there, friend," says Dog-Nose. "We're not trekking miles through any cold, wet anything. We're going to do this my way and outsmart that little sleaze once and for all, something I've been wanting to do ever since I met him."

And so Dog-Nose and I went into the trapping business in a somewhat unconventional sort of way, and instead of stocking up on traps and chain and baits and scents, we started collecting all the garbage in town in the back of Dog-Nose's Jeep and scattering it around the shoulders of blind curves on Highway 7 every evening just before dusk. Then every morning, just after sunup, we headed back out in the Jeep and picked up the raccoons, skunks, foxes, squirrels, rabbits, opossums, and even the occasional weasels and minks that had been attracted

57

to the garbage and knocked into Kingdom Kong by the night-time traffic coming around those curves.

Now I must admit that the scheme was not without its bugs. Every once in a while, we were met by a scene of such carnage and slaughter that left no doubt as to the fact that our poor quarry was unfortunately taken by the Grim Reaper driving a semi-trailer at seventy miles an hour. In such cases, we were forced to park the Jeep off the road and spend most of the morning picking through barely identifiable animal parts to see if anything at all could be salvaged of our night's work. Usually it meant going home without having accomplished much except for feeding the crows, but it often helped draw a new set of targets for the following night like no kind of garbage ever managed to do.

On good days, though, it was a simple matter of zigzagging back and forth across the road with Dog-Nose driving and me hanging out the other side door, scooping the bodies off the road with a snow shovel and tossing them into a garbage bag that we had held open around a frame in the back of the Jeep. Then we would go back home and work on the critters for the rest of the day, and when they were all skun out and set to drying, we would go collect some more garbage around town, throw in the innards from the day's work, and go back out to set our traps, as it were.

You might be thinking that this was a pretty disgusting way to be doing things. Well it turns out that a lot of folks think that way so you are not alone. But the fact is that it was not bad at all. Most of the time, the animals had just been hit and not run over and squished at all, leaving them in as good shape as if they had been shot, and it does not embarrass me any to say that most of them were in such good shape that we not only had near-perfect skins to send to Lematina, but we kept ourselves in meat for the entire time we were working on this project. You think that is unwholesome? Well it is no worse than shooting a moose and having to come back the next day with help to drag it out. That is day-old dead meat just the same, isn't it?

So we made a pretty good show of it, bringing in skins at a rate that was quite extraordinary by working different curves in the highway according to a carefully controlled schedule that Dog-Nose worked out based on species movement, population densities, moon phases, and other factors that Dog-Nose had a good solid handle on. Naturally, though, this good a thing was not destined to last forever, and it was that greedy weasel Lematina who finally ended up queering his own deal and hoisting his own petard.

You remember I told you that he had come up to our place just to find Dog-Nose and then had gotten into his car and driven off to parts unknown? Well, he had no more known that Dog-Nose was in the area than he knew I was. And he never heard of me before in his life. Yet the fact was, I was the one he came out to see on account of the fact that he was visiting every guide in the area and making the same "exclusive" deal for getting furs. But then here steps out of the door his old acquaintance from school, and the slicker makes out as how he came up looking for him just to offer this proposition. I have to hand it to him, the man was quicker on his feet than a tiger beetle, but that is not the half of it.

Now you cannot blame the man for wanting to cover all his bases. When you think of it, it was not likely that a couple of fellows like Dog-Nose and I could supply a whole fur business by ourselves no matter how good at it we were. So you figure he is going to get himself a few suppliers around the area. But what this snake did was to make the same "exclusive" deal with everybody and not tell any of us that we were all competing against our friends and neighbors, but only that he was getting better furs from somebody else in the area for cheaper prices. That is how he kept all our prices down and production up and made sure he had the area covered as well. Well, you can imagine what that kind of system did to the fur-bearing population around those parts. And you can bet that the better part of the guides in the area would have had nothing to do with that kind of decimation if they had known what was going on, least of all Dog-Nose and me. But we did not know because of Lematina keeping us in the dark from each other so we could not all form some kind of cartel and control our own prices against him.

So, pretty soon the production started to drop noticeably on account of the unbearable trapping pressure in the region, and the only method that was consistently bringing in furs was ours, which was not hampered by the conventional problems of overhunting, but was a more natural way of going about it (and you can bet that yes I do appreciate the so-called irony in that statement that I just made).

And before long, the greedy Lematina is complaining to one guide or another that how come Dog-Nose and Junior are still bringing in good quantities of pelts, and there went the cat out of the bag, which he no doubt would have skun out had he caught it. So now the jig is up, except that the way little minds work is a peculiar thing. You would think that once those fellows who had been exploited out of their pants and suckered into raping their own environments would, in the learning of it, turn on him who tricked them into it. But no. Instead of that, they all get together to take it out on those who did better at it than they did, which is me and Dog-Nose. Those one or two guides who heard Lematina let the cat out went back and told all the others except for us, on account of them perceiving us as the enemy for still doing well while they were doing lousy. And so they all decide to find out what we are up to.

Well, for idiots, they put together an elaborate plan for keeping an eye on us, and it did not take long for them to find out our system, especially since we did not realize that we had anything to hide from anybody and so were doing everything right out in the open anyway.

It is a funny thing how most people make such a big difference between an animal that is shot or trapped and one that is hit by a car. I still do not really understand it. But I can tell you that I have never seen anything before nor since like the size of the commotion and hoo-ha that developed when word got out that the Clothes Encounters of the Furred Kind stores were selling coats made from road-kill. Sonny Lematina was buried for so long under returned coats, subpoenas, summonses, citations, writs, mandates, fiats, warrants, law suits, and chapter elevens that we did not see him again until the trial.

I suppose it was our testimony at the trial that got him in trouble and saved his ass both at the same time, for what Dog-Nose and I told was the truth. We related how we had, in fact, been supplying Lematina with furs that had been technically road-kill, and so it was apparent that whether or not his customers were justified in their prejudice against road-kill clothing, they were definitely justified in their claim that they were wearing some. On the other hand, we also testified that as far as we knew, Lematina had no idea we were getting our furs by that method and so had no idea that he was selling furs that his customers might find objectionable, as they put it.

At any rate, the denouement was that Lematina was not guilty of anything illegal but was obligated to take back all the road-kill coats that nobody wanted and to give everybody back their money, which he had pretty much all spent. So he was in pretty serious trouble, anyway, and in danger of having to go to jail for non-complying and whatnot. And that was when he took to smuggling drugs.

But before I get to that, I should tell you that it was that trial more than anything that gave Dog-Nose and me the boost we needed to get our business off its butt. The publicity we got in the New York papers (which is where the trial was) was something to behold. Not only were there interviews with us as the star witnesses, which showed off Dog-Nose's depth of knowledge on wildlife and whatnot, but there was coverage of the magnificent oration that Dog-Nose gave at the trial about the real tragedy done to the environment by Lematina's greed and others like him. And, at the time, it was not the usual things to be heard from a fellow who made his living showing other people how and where to kill animals and fish. This was the kind of thinking that came as something fresh and newsworthy for the press, who you can bet made plenty hay with it. We could not have bought better advertising from anywhere for any money. And it was that occasion right there that started us off to success and that started Dog-Nose off to his destiny as the Legend, though I believe there was not another person at the time who had yet seen the glimmer of it except for myself.

We were in New York for two weeks, during which time I saw Dog-Nose only in the courtroom and during interviews. Every other minute, he was in the bedroom of one rich, gorgeous, and traumatized victim of Clothes Encounters of the Furred Kind or another, who had come to testify against Lematina. And every day I saw him in court, he was walking more and more like a fellow what had his privates borrowed for batting practice up at Yankee Stadium. But the smile on his face left no doubt as to how one man's limit is just another Legend's warm-up.

I, meanwhile, was not so much in demand by the bereaved, but did manage to service the occasional roommate to an extent that suited me fine and left me time to spend every other available minute in a tackle and gun shop that I discovered called Abercrombie & Fitch, the likes of which I have never dreamed of.

But getting back to Sonny Lematina, it was the exigencies of his situation as a result of the outcome of the trial that led him to out and out criminal activity in the form of smuggling drugs. Apparently it was something he observed on his return trip from Canada to New York, during the trip he made to set up the trapping arrangements, that gave him the idea. He was on the same plane with a party of sports who were returning from a salmon trip, and each of the sports had frozen his catch for taking it home. Following the sports through customs, Lematina observed that the frozen salmons all went through without a hitch and that, in fact, there is not much you can do to check a froze salmon anyway.

So Lematina set up a whole complicated organization involving the flying of heroin from Asia or somewheres to someplace in Canada. Then he would buy up all the fresh salmon he could get from guides and sports and whomever, and he would stuff packets of heroin down into the fish and freeze them solid. Then he and a bunch of lackeys would dress up like sports with salmon rods and tackle and whatnot like they had been salmon fishing, and they would bring the frozen salmons into New York, stuffed with drugs, and right through customs. All this was revealed through the newspaper accounts of Lematina's arrest and the subsequent breakup of the drug ring when the scam fell through.

Apparently he was wildly successful with this ploy for a good long time and naturally, on account of the sleazy way he was, he saw no reason to give up the good thing after he was all squared away with his obligations from the road-kill furs decision. So sooner or later he got caught, and it was as a result of an on-the-ball, salmon-fishing, customs officer who got into a friendly conversation with one of Lematina's phoney sports and got more than a little suspicious when the imbecile got real talky and started telling about his great fight with a thirty-pounder that broke off after his bobber got caught in the weeds.

But anyway, that stuffed salmon part was not really anything to do with Dog-Nose and me, but I thought you might like to hear it on account of you already knew who Sonny Lematina was. The important thing is how he very indirectly set us out on our course of celebrity, and so he is a necessary evil in the history of what this book is about.

After spending some short time in prison, Lematina

managed to get out on some legal technicality and went back into retailing again. As I recall, he had opened another store, this one selling ladies' powders and perfumes, that was located in the Head of the Sphinx Mall outside of Concord, New Hampshire. He was killed in an explosion there just before Christmas of 1968.

Anyway, here is another poem of Dog-Nose's that I found in the box, and I think it relates to the "trapping" episode that I have described in this chapter. Naturally, it is just as it came from the box, so do not blame me if it is no good.

THE SONG OF THE ROAD-KILL TRAPPER

Firestone fox, Cooper 'coon, Michelin mink on the
  pavement.
No self-mutilation, no springsteel bite, no long-endured
  enslavement.
Quick American murders, Detroit deaths. A bumper crop from
  FenderFurs.
From one soft shoulder to another they go, given to milady by a
  friend of hers.
Rounding the curves, smooth shifting and a steamy night on the
  blacktop.
Eighteen wheels-worth throbbing in the loins as he slides into the
  truckstop.
The waitress meets him in the john and hikes her skirt with
  laughter.
All other fur is safe tonight; it's beaver that he's after.

5
PROMOTING THE LEGEND

Well I'm sitting here thinking
Just how sharp I am.
I'm an under assistant west coast promo man.

— The Rolling Stones

I have never been much good at anything that might be construed as being in the greater category of what you call "business." The failed bakery was a dead testimony to the way I have always run things that were supposed to have the end result of making money. That is probably why the guiding business was doing so putrid once we set out to make it our sole means of support. While it was a matter of having a good time hunting and fishing and wandering around in the outdoors like I loved to do for the sheer enjoyment of it, things were booming. But as soon as it took on the makings of a business, it was goodnight ladies.

Dog-Nose did not seem too upset by the glaring failure of the enterprise, saying that it was just a matter of time before things got off its butt and people started hearing good things about us and came lining up at our door, as he put it, while meantime he was buried deep in books by day and in an assortment of female orifices by night. But it was beyond my understanding of the way things worked as to how in hell anybody was going to hear anything at all about us, good *or* bad, when there was not anybody doing the telling.

Well, that was something that was on my mind more or less all the time in those early days, and although I had no formal education on the subject, I seemed to sense by instinct that there must be something that existed that was a means to making things happen in a faster time from the normal drag-ass course of events under which we were laboring. Little did I know but that the whole goddam world is run on the very system that I was seeking.

It was the Clothes Encounters of the Furred Kind trial with its attendant publicity that gave me the spark I needed to discover in myself a talent that I can honestly say was to change the course of our business, our lives, and the folklore of North America. It was as though it had been hiding inside me from birth and was growing and learning and developing itself inside me for just that time when I was to discover the need for it and put it to use. That is exactly the way it seemed, and it was that image that makes me wonder what would have happened if I did not ever discover it and let it out. Possibly it would have kept right on growing and developing like a blowfly cyst or something and got bigger than my whole self until finally there was no more room for it and it just exploded all over the inside of my clothes and shoes and on down into my socks like a month-long case of the shortsteps I once had from drinking some water that turned out to have a dead beaver upstream from it.

But, anyway, that did not happen, and I let it out in time to find out that it was exactly what we needed. Just those few interviews and articles that were done right away during the trial, and then the way it was picked up by some other papers and magazines, were enough to attract some attention to us and bring in a few sports that had seen the write-ups and wanted to meet the subjects on account of being impressed with the sound of Dog-Nose. And it was then that I got the inkling of the enormous potential in Dog-Nose's personality and of the prodigious power of bullshit.

I slept on that for a good few weeks, not in one long sleep of course, but what I mean to say is that it was constantly on my mind for a good long time, and I began to see clearly how I had fallen into the secret center of the way things work. What it was all about was getting your name out, and if you had to bend the truth a little to get it heard, then you bent it, and after awhile it did not matter at all if the bends were lies because the name took on a life of its own and the rest of the world did the lying for you. And if it was done right, with just enough strategically placed truth to back up the strategically placed nonsense, nobody would care after a while which was which, and fame and celebrity would be standing in your kitchen. Naturally this whole plan had to have the right ingredients and timing, but I figured we were better than halfway there just on account of Dog-Nose being Dog-Nose, and the rest was up to me.

Once that flashlight had gone off in my head, it was like somebody had finally opened the windows on a perfect spring morning after they had been closed tight all winter in a tiny cabin where you and six dogs has all been cooking, sweating, and farting for six months. That is when I finally felt some great self-confidence blow over me like a rush of fresh air and finally told Dog-Nose about the whole thing.

You cannot blame him for being skeptical. Here was a fellow who had pitifully little education and nothing but failures in all his business endeavors, telling a well-schooled and eloquent fellow of good breeding that I was going to turn the business around by way of a new-found but untried (which so far boils down to "imagined") talent for promotion and public relations. I suppose I myself would have laughed, too, although probably with a lot less derision.

"Where do you suddenly come off being such a public relations strategist," says Dog-Nose with a face full of scorn. "You barely have a passing acquaintance with the English language, yet you're standing here telling me that you're single-handedly planning our deliverance from penury. Did you recently have a brain transplant of which I am unaware?"

"Up yours, numbnuts," I say, not particularly appreciating his insinuations. "Just because you have a good deal of book-learning and an undeniably charming command of the language, that does not mean your ideas are any better than mine. I am perfectly prepared to prove to you that I have a God-given talent for promotion that can benefit us both beyond our wildest dreams if you will but hear me out and give me your patronizing cooperation for once. Besides that, I do not exactly feel overwhelmed by the brilliance and abundance of the ideas coming out of *your* pompous brain."

"My apologies, Junior. You're absolutely right," he says with that winning way of his that first makes you feel like something he just stepped in and then, just as sincerely, makes you feel as though he is truly sorry and feels terrible and alone and at your mercy for friendship and love. "I have no talent myself for such things, and I am in fact more than a little uncomfortable with the prospect that your rough and untrained mind may prove to be our salvation. But, having brought that to the fore, I feel I can now deal with it. You have my full cooperation; our future is in your hands. What's on your mind?"

Dealing with Dog-Nose was always a lot like mistakenly taking a big bite of a moose turd and finding that you actually liked the taste of it. I do not know any other way to explain it.

"Look," I say, "you have any friend or relative who can be trusted and who lives someplace like Michigan or Altoona?"

"How about Buffalo?" he says. "I've got an old college chum named Fensterwald who has a law practice in Buffalo."

"Your old chums ain't been exactly proving to be all that trustworthy," I say, referring to Sonny Lematina, and he knew it.

"Lematina was not a chum, not from college, and not a lawyer. Don't start condemning everyone I know just because of one unfortunate acquaintance."

"Okay, we will go with your lawyer friend," I say. "All he has to do is mail something for us anyway." And I proceeded to tell Dog-Nose what I had in my mind.

I told him how I had been reading a recent issue of one of the hunting and fishing magazines that he had subscriptions to, and that there was an article about speckled trout fishing in Maine that gave the reader some pretty high hopes for a grand time, no holds barred.

"Actually, it sounds like a lot of overblown crap to me," I say, "but I think we can use it and go it one better in our favor. It ain't much, but we have got to start somewheres."

"Of course it's somewhat hyperbolized," says Dog-Nose. "You know as well as I that no trip can be as ideal as those articles make them out to be. That stuff is just another form of the promotional tripe of which you have lately become so enamored."

"I know that," I say, finding it hard to believe that he is thinking that he is teaching me something I have not already figured out. "And now you are going to write a very simple letter, signed with some phony moniker, that tells how you were reading that Maine article and was reminded of an even better trip that you took to Nova Scotia where you were guided by the best guide you ever had in your life."

And that is exactly what he did. Here is a copy of it that I cut out of the magazine and kept ever since:

In your June issue, you ran an article about brook trout fishing in Maine by John Swensen, which called to mind a similar, though perhaps better, trip I recently made to Nova Scotia. There, I was guided by a fellow for whom, I feel certain, the attainment of legendary stature as a guide and sportsman is only a matter of time. Many of your readers will cast an incredulous eye at Swensen's claims of having caught "well over a hundred wild brookies in an afternoon," but I do not. In fact, I can only express regret at his poor luck. W.C. Cooper, my matchless guide, introduced me to a pond in which I caught more than twice that number, finally giving up early from the pain in my shoulder caused by lifting so many five-pounders into the boat. Thanks to Swensen for his reminiscent piece.

A.H. Putnam
Buffalo, N.Y.

Then we put it in an envelope addressed to the magazine, and we sent it in another envelope to Fensterwald in

Buffalo so he could mail it to the magazine from there, and it would have the Buffalo postmark on it and look authentic.

That tiny little bit of brilliance brought us so much business that it was not until six months later that we had time or need to continue the strategy. You figure that magazine has got about a million or so readers. Maybe a half of them bother to read the letters in front. Maybe three-quarters of those give a fart about trout. Maybe a tenth of those are actually about to get up someday and go to Canada to do some trout fishing. Maybe one out of a hundred of those is going to remember about that letter and try to get in touch with us. And maybe a tenth of those letters are actually going to get to us. That comes to thirty-seven and a half sports, and the thirty-five sports that did in fact call us as a direct result of that letter makes my figuring about as good as you can get. Dog-Nose was duly impressed, and although he still mostly treated me like I was some inferior form of life, I could tell that he began to defer to my judgement in matters of promotion.

One thing you have probably noticed about that letter is that there is no mention of yours truly. That was a particular that came quite naturally to Dog-Nose in the writing of it, which I expected, but it was also a calculated decision that I finally came to myself. The way my figuring went was this: One. My whole purpose in this was to make myself some money doing what I liked doing, which was guiding and spending my time outdoors hunting and fishing. Two.

Whether I did that by myself or with Dog-Nose, I was in for doing most of the undesirable work of hauling and cooking and setting up camp anyway as well. Three. I am not one who flourishes in the so-called limelight, nor have I got what it takes to carry it off. Four. As long as I am in partnership with Dog-Nose Cooper, I am going to get my fair share of the take, no question. Five. The more famous he gets, the richer I get.

It was that kind of thinking that led me to realize how I got just as much benefit from only him becoming a Legend. And it would be a lot easier and less complicated to pull it off. So I made up my mind right there that in most cases it was better off leaving mention of Junior Fraser out of the picture.

The next step was obvious to me. If we could get thirty-five sports out of a one-paragraph letter that is buried in the front of the magazine, what kind of avalanche of inquiries was hiding in the impact of a whole article? So I got Dog-Nose to make up a piece that put all the elements of those barely believable outdoor stories into one terrific advertisement disguised as a fishing article. Naturally it had to be just right. If it sounded too hokey, those magazine people would see right through it. But then again, if it was not full of razzle-dazzle and Dog-Nose's name all over it (actually W.C. Cooper on account of Dog-Nose was not Dog-Nose yet), then why bother? So I had Dog-Nose write it, and then I pushed and poked it a bit and had him rewrite it here and there, and damn if it was not published. I will not make you read the whole of it, on account of you can get the gist from a few selected paragraphs, but it was a wild success. I am not going to tell you how many queries it turned up either until you finish, but I will bet you you do not guess even close. Here is how it started:

THE BASS AND BROOKIE TWO-STEP
by A.H. Putnam

The lake was a perfect mirror of the sky, and the spruces, black against the dawn, formed the rim of our universe. My guide, W.C. Cooper, sent our canoe gliding across the surface as smoothly as milkweed fluff blown across the winter ice. Cooper's handling of that canoe, unbeknownst to me at the time, was to exemplify his extraordinary expertise in every aspect of our outing, from the flies he gave me to use, exquisitely tied by himself, to his knowledge of the lake, the natural history of the area, and the fish.

And did we catch fish! Wild, pink-fleshed brookies, called speckled brook trout by the Nova Scotians who take justifiable pride in their magnificent fishery, rose to our flies with such frequency and regularity that it was barely full light before we had caught far more than could be eaten in a week. And the fighting spirit of the things! It was as if the wildness of the landscape had infused those finny creatures with a recklessness akin to hysteria. Yet, in comparison to the smallmouth bass in those waters, the hefty brookies seemed as tame as hatchery trout.

Yes, smallmouth, too! Bass that hit our flies with such vigor and fought with such unleashed fury that they spent more time out of the water than in. And they were in no less abundance than the trout, though in a different part of the lake, which Cooper knew better than I know the back of my own hand.

It went on like this for some ways, talking about specific flies that do not actually exist but which I had Dog-Nose make up the names of so the sports reading it would think they could not simply come up to Nova Scotia and catch fish without getting in touch with Dog-Nose and his special flies. And it talked about the excitement of catching specific fish:

> As I inched the beautifully tied Gluscap Crayfish fly across the rockpile, my arm was nearly jolted out of its socket. Never had a strike come with such ferocity, and as the silver surface of the lake shattered in an explosion of crystal shards, the six-pound bass rocketed into the air and hung a full ten seconds, walking on its tail in a fury of scaled savagery. I had never before been joined to such a fish as this. For the next quarter-hour, we were locked in a contest that had no predictable outcome. Yet, thanks to the wise and patient council of Cooper, I finally saw my prize expertly scooped up in his landing net.

If you have put on your hip boots in order to wade through this manure then you have definitely gotten the gist. And once again we sent it off to Dog-Nose's lawyer friend in Buffalo for forwarding to New York City, which is where the magazine was officed.

Now you can go ahead and try to guess the number of queries we got from that article's being published. If you are thinking dozens, you have got some more thinking to do.

Hundreds? No, not hardly. The answer is one. That is correct. Just one. And here is how that happened.

There is no A.H. Putnam in Buffalo. So when all those sports read the article and got all het up about how to get in touch with this Cooper fellow and all, they naturally wrote letters to the magazine asking how to find him. Well, the magazine did not have any better idea about how to find W.C. Cooper themselves. Apparently, the fellow in the letters department, who had helped everybody find us last time, did not work there any more, and nobody else had any notion of where to find us. So they put all the query letters in a big box and mailed it to A.H. Putnam in Buffalo, along with the payment check for writing the article. Naturally we never got the box full of letters nor the check neither on account of some pretty obvious reasons, and so it would appear that my brilliant plans for fame and fortune had blown up right in our face.

But there was one fellow, and I will not mention his name on account of he is still working for that same magazine even after all these years, that was the fishing editor of the magazine. And he was not about to be stopped by anything in the finding of W.C. Cooper.

It was he who got the magazine to hire a famous private eye to hunt down Dog-Nose and me. And you probably recall the great bruhaha that the magazine pulled off in a genius publicity stunt of its own when it announced that it had located "the great W.C. Cooper." I recall how, at the time, Dog-Nose likened it to Stanley's discovery of Livingstone, though I did not then know what he meant but do now. This was truly the turning point for us, for it was so much in the interest of the magazine to justify and get the most return from the expense of hiring the detective, that it went way the hell overboard in its glorification of Dog-Nose and the finding out of his whereabouts.

Ironically, it did take some doing for that gumshoe to ferret us out, though we were in no way hiding. In fact, the whole point of my plan was to get us discovered, and we were doing everything we could in that regard short of sending up flares and hiring a brass band.

Anyway, the private eye found us, and the magazine made the most of it, and that editor came up to spend some time being guided by us and interviewing us and then going back and writing about Dog-Nose for us, right in the very magazine that we had been conning with the phoney article and letter.

It was during his week with us when it came out that the magazine got a boxful of queries to A.H. Putnam's article (had we read it? "Oh, sure. Good piece. Nice fellow. Good time. Right. Right. Right. Right." etcetera) but that they had never been able to get in touch with him so that he could respond to the queries. But this editor fellow says that since he now knows how to find Dog-Nose, he will write that information up in his column so all those curious sports will have the information.

Well, all that did it, like I said. We would not have

ever had to write a single other article in order to get all the work we needed for the rest of our lives, what with word of mouth being such a successful factor in this business. But I was not satisfied. I had started on a course of making a Legend out of Dog-Nose, and it had got stuck in my curiosity as to whether I could actually make it work.

So I continued on my course of strategy with Dog-Nose's full cooperation, on account of he did not mind too much being turned into a Legend, and I had him write at least one fishing or hunting article each season under the name of A.H. Putnam that were always bigger-than-life adventures and claims about how great his guide W.C. Cooper was. And sure enough, each time an article came out, more and more queries came to the magazine, and the editors would write about how those readers could get in touch with Dog-Nose, and before too many months, Dog-Nose was becoming a Legend just from the sheer numbers of people who were trying to book his services.

Then, of course, there was the fortuitous incident that took place to change his name to Dog-Nose, which I have already written about in what is now Chapter 1. And you can bet your Purdy shotgun and all your Leonard rods on how that did not do the Legend plan any great harm. In addition to all that, I made certain to take snapshots of any really great trophy fish or buck or bear or whatever that one of our sports might take so as to use them as news releases at appropriate times, and you might remember seeing some of those with

Dog-Nose and one famous writer or politician or millionaire or another, holding some trophy whatever. They were all taken by me and sent around to the papers for maximum effect. I also seem to recall letting out a few dozen fictitious news pieces to the local rags that were picked up by AP, UPI, and whatall other wire services and fed verbatim to the big city papers. They were all innocent enough; things like "Famous Guide Tracks and Finds Lost Child," "Rampaging Bear Tranquilized by Guide," "Guide Rescues Woman from Certain Death," and like that. They were always short and to the point without too many facts to disprove. About 90 percent of the folk stories that have built up around the Dog-Nose Legend have their roots in those releases. And I do not mind telling that they were actually my so-called fabrications on account of they have done nobody any harm. So what if they were not entirely true? They have now fallen peacefully into the realm of folklore or art or literature or whatever, and are a part of America, God bless her.

The rest, as some writers have said, is history. The man did become a Legend in his own time. As a matter of fact, he was a Legend *early* in his own time. And you can see how that came about.

(By the way, if there is any reader out there who happens to have the name A.H. Putnam and is of about the right age to pull off the scam, you might want to make a go of getting some of those checks that that magazine never paid out. Tell them you used to live in Buffalo but traveled around alot.)

Unfortunately I have not been able to find anything in the box that Dog-Nose wrote relevant to this chapter, but in digging out that letter and article that he wrote for the magazine, I came across a funny thing that you might enjoy, and they were written during this time that I have been writing about.

One day while nothing much is going on, Dog-Nose is scribbling away and hands me this poem:

There once was a fellow named Jr.
Who would haul you to court and start sr.
He'd hire a lawyer
Who'd come gunnin' fawyer,
And the settlement surely would rr.

"It is, of course, a nonsense limerick," he says. "By that I mean that the content has no basis in reality. It is, rather, the clever extension of the jay-ar peculiarity as the abbreviation for junior wherein lies the wit. But I suppose I'll have to explain it to you."

"Why don't you just let me wallow in my own ignorance for a while," I say to him. "Maybe I will scrape enough brain cells together to figure it out on my own in a couple of months."

And with that I turn over the scrap of paper and write

the following, handing it back to him in about a minute:

> A reply from the fellow named Jr.:
> Be careful you don't end up scrr.
> Cojones away,
> 'Cause then you can't play
> With the ladies, you great big babr.

He was impressed.

6
WOMEN

Ob-La-Di, Ob La-Da,
Life goes on,
Bra.

— The Beatles

On rereading the last chapter that I have written (Chapter 5) I am forced to come to the conclusion that I have been doing a lot of what you might call blowing on my own horn. At least you could easily construe it as that, though in fact it is actually a necessary and inevitable episode in the truthful and complete telling of the Dog-Nose story, which is what this book is supposed to be about after all. How am I supposed to give you an accurate picture of the life and time of one Dog-Nose Cooper, Legendary Guide, if I do not explain the so-called underlying factors that brought him to his celebrated stature?

And if those factors involved a heavy dosage of the behind-the-scenes manipulations of one Junior Fraser who is your writer and narrator, then those things must be told without any varnish. It is no time for false modesty nor humility when a true picture is to be written. And so I make no excuses nor apologies for what I said in Chapter 5. That is the last I will say about it.

The reason I wrote that last paragraph (above) is to ward off those critics who will no doubt have something to say about how I am trying to steal some of Dog-Nose's glory now that he is dead and gone and has no more say about it than a spent shell. I still painfully recall the harsh letters I received from various quarters after the appearance of Chapter 1, which was published, as you recall, as a separate article and which caused the whole chain of events that led to the writing of this whole book. Those letters were anything but complimentary, and they mainly complained about this very thing that is worrying me now. But to them I have this to say: If you are more in love with a lot of made-up crap than you are with the Truth, then you are a low-life slime for whom I have no more regard than something that crawls out from under the stinking remains of something that even the skunks and buzzards will not eat. And let that be the end of it.

That said, I can move on to tell more about the Legend. Everybody who has not had large parts of his brain removed knows about Dog-Nose's illustrious affairs with the ladies. Some of them have filtered down into the same folklore realms as his most famous hunting and fishing exploits, especially the one about Dog-Nose and the Governor's wife spending three days and nights in a spruce tree on account of a trophy blackie lying in wait below. I do not wish to disillusion anybody about this one by telling how it was actually yours truly in a bearskin for sixty of those seventy-odd hours, shuffling and snorting and scared to death that the real bear was going to return after Dog-Nose recognized what a good thing he had going and talked me into continuing the charade until Mrs. — — - had had her fill of her Tarzan and Jane fantasy. All I will say is that some of those famous stories had a bit more to them than what met the public eye, as it were.

Like the one about how Dog-Nose saved that famous actress from drowning while river-fishing for smallmouth in the upper Kennebec. I am sure that unless you were lost in the jungles of Fuji at the time, you remember the photographs that were splashed all over the tabloids showing a dripping wet Dog-Nose with his shirt torn open, carrying a soaked Ms. — — - from the river with her arms around his neck, a look of utter gratitude and adoration on her face, and some strategically placed wet tresses over the front pocket of a quite transparent drenched blouse. Just how do you think there happened to be a photographer on the spot in the nick of time?

Well, the truth is that there was not any near drowning and there was not any life-saving neither. The fact is that the actress in question had not come up to go fishing for smallmouth any more than a bass has fleas. And it did not take long to realize how it was Dog-Nose that was the real quarry.

Before all this Legend status befell Dog-Nose, I have to admit that I was as innocent about women as the proverbial babe and the woods. I guess I had my fair share of what you might call your carnal experiences with the fair sex, but it was always something that I had to work for, if you know what I mean. I was not the kind of man that women exactly threw themselves at. Consequently, my experiences in this regards were of the more conventional variety. The kinds of things that were common practice to Dog-Nose was a whole new eye-opener to me.

As I have been trying to relate in past chapters, Dog-Nose was a natural woman magnet even before his Legend days. The same unfathomable qualities that made men and boys look to him as a genuine hero type made women and girls get ideas the likes of which they did not know they could possess, nor me neither. Which is why Dog-Nose took as normal the uninhibited behavior of women, while the things I was to witness almost daily while in partnership with him never ceased to leave me gaping in sweaty wonder.

Anyway, I am telling you this because I suspect as how most of you are closer to the experience of myself than to Dog-Nose when it comes to matters of dalliance, and so you may not believe the kinds of dormant passions Dog-Nose routinely aroused in even the most ordinary-looking ladies, passions that manifested themselves in the most immodest goddam behavior you have never seen.

The movie actress who I started talking about some paragraphs back is what you call your case in point. Here was a gal who had no intention of doing anything in the great outdoors except dropping her drawers, and her particular obsession was doing things with Dog-Nose while standing up in a canoe. God is my witness.

This particular fixation was not of the least surprise to Dog-Nose, for as I have tried to impress on you, he had just about seen it all (and done it, too) since he was out of puberty. So he and the actress would arise early and set out on the river in the canoe, and I do not know all of what went on for all those hours spent outdoors, but every evening while I was preparing supper, the two of them would come dripping into camp with the actress in Dog-Nose's arms and a dreamy smile on her face, and I would have to hike a mile or two downriver to fetch the canoe that they had finally swamped in the throes of their debauchery.

This went on for a few days by which time I finally came up with a way to make hay from this whole adventure without getting sued nor having to pay for it neither. One evening near the end of the lady's scheduled stay, I loaded my camera and had it all ready to go when they came squishing into camp. I snapped a couple of nice shots of the happy couple with the river in the background and the spruces all framing them like a church door.

"Just what the hell do you think you're doing, you little turd?" screams the actress all het up to beat the band.

"It is customary," I say in my sweetest tone, "for me to present our clients with a picture of themself with their trophy catch. But it is beginning to look as how you ain't about to catch nothing but a cold, so I thought you might like a picture of you and your trophy catch."

She softens some and says, "Mind your own goddam business, lackey."

But Dog-Nose suspects that I am up to something that is ultimately to our mutual benefit, and he steps in to soothe the situation.

"That's very nice of you, Junior," he says, "and we'll be sure to send Ms. —— - a framed and autographed copy as soon as we have the film processed. Why don't you get into some dry clothes, dear, and we'll sample some of Junior's haute cuisine?"

And she goes off to her tent as docile and agreeable as a tamed doe, batting her long lashes and wiggling her lovely behind as though she were not a nasty and unlikable bitch after all.

"What have you got on that devious mind of yours?" Dog-Nose whispers to me after she has slogged safely off to a distance. "I'll have no part of any blackmail scheme, if that's what you're planning."

"You got a goddam lot of nerve suggesting such low

behavior," I hiss at Dog-Nose. "Besides, how the hell am I going to be blackmailing somebody with photographs like this when the whole world already knows she has come up here specifically to go fishing with the great Dog-Nose Cooper? It is a good thing you ain't handling the business end of this outfit on account of with that kind of half-assed thinking we would be broke and in jail both."

After that low blow, which I still think he deserved, Dog-Nose put one of those looks on his face that expressed a multitude of emotions, not the least of which was the "although-you-have-hurt-me-to-the-quick-I-will-remain-your-loyal-and-true-friend" one, plus a "if-not-that,-then-what?" kind of question. But before I had time to answer, the actress came out of her tent all dried and changed and it was time for me to go serve the oats and beans, or whatever it was that Dog-Nose said in French.

Well, what I did with those photos, of course, was to send a copy to every one of those New York papers with a press release that explained how Dog-Nose had made a dramatic and life-saving rescue of the actress after she capsized the canoe while trying to land a trophy smallie. What was she going to do, deny my story and tell them the truth? Here was a way of adding yet more notoriety to the Dog-Nose Legend by both associating him with celebrities, showing how he can get them onto trophy fish, and adding a little daring-do to the whole shebang.

And did it ever work like a charm. Hell, it was *better*

than blackmail.

Still, though, there were unquestionably two sides to the notoriety coin, especially where women were concerned, for it was not too far down into our prime years together that things began to take a turn toward the dangerous in that regard. I have never seen so many husbands and wives wanting to shoot each other and using a hunting trip as an excuse to do it. Worse yet, as far as Dog-Nose was concerned, was the utter convenience of your basic cuckolded husband scenario. There was not anything, in the mind's eye of the general public, like a secluded wilderness camp for offering endless opportunities for hanky-panky between the luscious young bride of some fat old millionaire and the notoriously randy womanizing Legend. And there is not any jury alive that would doubt the likelihood of said fatcat finding cause to send both wife and guide to their just desserts with his prized shotgun, one barrel for each of them, over and under.

Dog-Nose always said it came from reading too much Hemingway, but I do not think it has got anything to do with too much anything but rather with too little, and I cautioned him to the point of nagging as to the dangers of his position.

"I deeply appreciate your concern, old friend," says Dog-Nose on more than a dozen occasions, "but you may rest assured that I am well aware of my precarious position and have come to fully appreciate the equivalent emotions of the hooked worm."

I took that to mean that he was feeling like a piece of

bait at times, but I was hard pressed to figure who was doing the baiting and who was being baited. It was clear, on occasion, as how a neglected wife was making no secret of cozying up to Dog-Nose so as to arouse the jealousy and rekindle the interest of her young but marriage-altered buck. That kind of situation was no real threat to anybody on account of how it was so obvious and Dog-Nose could intervene on the behalf of both parties and make each see they were meant for each other. Dog-Nose, after all, was a pretty good marriage counsellor on account of his background of psychology classes in college, and he was a caring and compassionate human being as well. In cases like that, of which there were plenty, Dog-Nose was always more than happy to bring the grateful couple together to their original state of matrimonial bliss after taking his plea-sure with the distaff side a time or two, of course.

But the really menacing predicaments were the ones involving the old husbands and the horny wives. Those women was made both foolish and spiteful by carnal neglect and tended to throw all subtlety to the wind. Their one goal was to get back at a husband who could not or would not give them what Dog-Nose could and to make no bones about it. Here is where a "Legend in His Own Time" can fast lose four fifths of his title.

Although we were running up against that kind of thing about as often as we ran across chipmunks in camp, there is one incident that sticks out and begs for the telling.

It involved a fellow and his wife who I will call the

W____s on account of I do not care to be sued. My impression is that they were not overly rich. But she was not to be outdone in the expense and quality of the equipment that she brought along. His gear, though, was of no particular distinction. He was not even especially happy about being there, for he was clearly not of the caliber of his wife when it came to fishing and shooting. All this W____ gent could talk about was his work, which I seem to recall had something to do with the stock market or some other area of manipulating somebody else's money to the point where it increases enough to take a piece of it for yourself.

All those facts, added to the lady's behavior toward Dog-Nose and away from W____, brought me to seeing clearly as how the missus was a widow to the husband's work and as how the husband was in the habit of trying to make up for it by buying her the best possible gear that fit her interests. And that was supposed to take the place of intimacy. She, meanwhile, was clearly well versed in matters of coquetry as an equal and opposite reaction to her husband's disregard, as it were. Basically, there was nothing new in that. We had seen variations on the same theme a hundred times. But what made this one so treacherous was the brooding personality of W____. He was not totally oblivious of the whole problem like so many other men, and he was not aware but tolerant of it neither. He knew the score all right, but it made him mean and driven. He wanted out, and he was desperate and at the end of his rope.

All that left Dog-Nose at the end of the hook again, and we both saw that real clearly within a couple of days of being with this pair.

It was late in September, and they had come up for moose. That is to say that *she* came up for moose; he came up to brood. It was clear to us from the start that he was not the hunter in the family, that he was not happy about being away from his work, particularly to be up in the sticks on a moose hunt, and that something was up. One evening in camp, while the missus was down on the river fishing for trout and W_____ was reading in his tent, I and Dog-Nose got a chance to put our heads together and see what we each were thinking.

"The man is so obviously not enjoying himself," says Dog-Nose, "that his presence here is particularly striking. I would have taken this fellow as the type who is so engrossed in his work as to have simply sent his wife off on this trip while remaining, himself, in the city."

"My thoughts, exactly," I say. "The fellow can't shoot worth a spit, never stops thinking about work, clearly can't control his wife's activities whether indoors or out so his being here or not being here doesn't make no difference, and he doesn't seem to be making no attempt at working things out in no way I can see."

"Well, following the deductive reasoning of Sherlock Holmes, which goes something to the effect that once you eliminate the impossible, whatever remains, however improbable, must be the truth, we can proceed along the following lines," says Dog-Nose. "He is not here to hunt moose, nor enjoy himself, nor to get away from work, nor to chaperon his wife, nor to improve their relationship. Are we agreed?"

"Yeah, but I still cannot believe that the only possibility we have got left is that he is along to kill his wife," I say, seeing the direction his thinking is going and stealing his punchline.

"Then give me another reason," Dog-Nose says too loud so we have to hunker down and drop into shhhhhhushes and whispers for fear of W____ catching our drift.

"Well, hell, I don't know," say I. "There could be a million reasons we ain't thought of. We don't know the man from atoms. Maybe he has got some kind of weird thing for snuggling into the body cavities of fresh-gutted mooses. Maybe he can only get it up with his wife right after she kills something. Maybe he has got some rare disease that can only be cured by his eating the ground gall-stones of a fresh-killed moose. Maybe his granny were killed by a moose and he likes to watch people kill them back. Maybe he has got some kind of....."

"You are, of course, quite right," interrupts Dog-Nose, "but what's your true visceral feeling about this, partner?"

"My gut tells me," I say, "that this whacko is fixing to shoot the wife. And what really worries me is that he either is going to miss and shoot you, or that you are already part of the plan anyway."

"Right," says Dog-Nose, taking charge again, "and here

is the way I see this scenario unfolding. Tomorrow I will take Mrs. W____ out to look for our quarry. If W____ declines my invitation and opts to stay in camp, you stay back as well and keep an eye on him. Tail him if he goes anywhere. If he decides to come along, I'll guide the missus, and you stick with W____. Watch him like a snake."

"Wait a minute," I say. "Why don't I take the lady and you stick with W____? That way he can't shoot you and her at the same time and make it look like he caught you two in the act."

"There are a lot of reasons, Junior," he says with that look that makes you feel like you have just got the same easy arithmetic question wrong again for the nineteenth time in a row. "First of all, this fellow is clearly going ahead with his plan despite all difficulties. The easier we make it for him, the more likely we will be able to anticipate his move. The harder we make it, the more likely he will catch us by surprise."

"With your pants down, as it were," I mumble under my breath. But Dog-Nose lets it pass.

"We also don't want to make him feel that he has to kill all of us, for Heaven's sake. So let's keep it simple and just hold a close eye on him. Besides, Mrs. W____ insists that I attend her, personally."

"Roger," I say.

"Attend," says Dog-Nose, annoyed.

"No, I mean 'over-and-out,'" I say.

The next morning dawned a queer foggy gray with the fall leaves glowing through the mist, nothing short of the perfect calendar setting for a day when a legendary guide is to take a lady on a moose hunt while the danger of getting murdered by her deranged husband looms over the landscape like the weather itself. This was the way it always was with Dog-Nose. Not only were the women always ready to cooperate, but the weather had a way of building him Hollywood sets as a backdrop for his life. You know those skies that suddenly break open to send fanned beams of sunlight out from wild, rolling thunderheads like there is no question but that God himself is up there playing the organ? Well I have never in all my life seen so many of them showing up at the most remarkable times until I hooked up with Dog-Nose, not to mention rainbows, lightning bolts, thunder claps, downpours, sudden dead-calm breaks in the wind. It was like the man walked around with his own personal special effects department hiding in the trees.

"Mrs. W_____ and I are going to bag a trophy today, sir," says Dog-Nose to W_____, who has pulled his folding chair out of the tent and is reading, his back to the rest of us, under a hemlock by the river. "Perhaps you would like to accompany us."

Without turning around, W_____ just waves his hand like he was brushing away a fly and keeps right on reading. Dog-Nose gives me a quick nod of the head that is really more like a toss of the chin and that means I am to keep a careful eye on this character on account of we are giving him plenty of rope and he has now the perfect opportunity to make his move. Then the guide and the lady fold off into the woods.

I continue straightening up around the camp, sweeping out the tents, washing pots and cooking-gear, gathering firewood, and generally looking like I am busy even after I have finished doing everything necessary for twice as long as it actually takes. But W____ is killing time, too. He does not know that I know this, but I do, for I have been keeping a corner of my eye on him during the doing of my chores. I notice that he is looking like he is reading, but he has not turned any pages in the last twenty minutes. Either he is the slowest reader on Earth, he has fallen asleep, or he is not reading at all, but just putting on appearances.

Well, I know he is not a slow reader on account of I have watched how fast he reads when he is really reading, and that is not the least bit slow. And I know he is not sleeping on account of the way his fingers of the hand that is not holding the book are drumming on the arm of his chair. That is not a thing that one does in his sleep. So that left stalling, scheming, brooding, or all three, all of which pointed to bad road ahead.

After what seemed like forever but was only about a half-hour, W____ gets up out of his chair and stretches his arms and shakes out his legs and plops his book down on the chair.

"Anything I can get for you, Mr. W____?" I ask.

"No thank you, Junior," he says with uncharacteristic

cordiality and animation, "I think I'll just stretch my legs a bit and mosey on down to the stream." And he heads off into the woods in the wrong direction.

"Mosey" was not one of the words I would have expected from this character, but since it was the first time I had heard him string more than two words and a grunt together this whole trip, I cannot rightly say how he would have normally talked anyway. In addition to that, his heading off in the wrong direction did not mean anything, either. He would not know which way the water lay if you had drawn him a map, on account of he had not set foot out of camp yet during his whole stay and probably did not know how to read a map anyhow.

Before following him, I duck back into my tent to grab my rifle, when I find to my extreme shock that it was not there. And suddenly the nasty truth of the whole plot dawns on me like ice water down the shorts as I realize how my partner and best friend is supposed to get shot by my own gun, and me made to look like I did it. I was not clear as to how W____ was going to work that out, but with my rifle gone it was plain to me that that was his intention. Quick as I can, I unpack my spare, grab some ammunition, and sneak off after W____.

I catch sight of him about a hundred yards from camp where he is stopped in a little hollow. I hunker down beside a hemlock and watch and wait, and I see him lift up a mat of brush he has piled up to hide something underneath. Sure enough, there is my rifle. When in hell he took it out of my tent and snuck off to stash it, I have not the foggiest idea. And what is more, he has also got himself what looks like a little radio and a pair of headsets under there that he is unwrapping from a plastic bag. He puts on the headphones, snaps on the radio, and points the antenna around in all directions, homing in finally on the direction that I know Dog-Nose and Mrs. W____ to have gone off in.

Well, after putting one thing together with another, I felt like I have just backed into a porcupine. Here I had been thinking that I had nothing to worry about from this fellow after he has given Dog-Nose and his wife a half-hour lead on account of how there is no way in hell he has the wherewithal to ever figure out where they have headed. Now I find that he has apparently planted some kind of beeper on his wife somehow and is tracking her like the Wildlife Service tracks tagged bears. Not only that, he has my gun. With all this many surprises, I am beginning to suspect the man might even be able to shoot a lot better than he has led us on to believe. And that was a scary thought on account of it meant I might actually have to shoot him first if he was to draw a bead on Dog-Nose.

But I soon enough began to realize that I probably did not have to worry too much about his shooting ability if his woodsmanship was any indication of that sort of thing, for although he was smart and crafty, it was all in a pretty mechanical sort of way that showed a serious lack of savvy to things natural. The heartless son of a bitch was following his wife's signal on a beeline, and I had no choice but to follow.

For the next two hours and a half, the two of us (with me only about twenty yards behind on account of he could not hear me with his earphones on) bushwacked through swamps, bogs, marshes, fens, and every form of lowland wetland mess ever created. We ripped our way through alder hells and shredded ourselves in tangles of briar. We climbed over and under the worst nightmare of deadfalls and blowdowns that has ever collected itself this side of the river Styx. And all because this fool did not know how to follow a signal any other way but straight at it. Before too long it was all I could do to keep from blasting the bastard just for putting me through all that. To me it would have been a clear case of self-defense, but I was still lucid enough to realize that I would have to drag the whole jury and judge out there to make them believe it. Meanwhile, W____ was forging ahead with the strength of his deadly convictions.

Pretty soon he slows up some, and I could tell by the way he is swinging that little radio back and forth that we are coming close to his quarry. His movements started to take on the look of stealth, but in a goofy exaggerated way like a kid playing at spies. Here was one unsprung whacko.

I spotted Dog-Nose and the lady long before W____ did. He was using his gizmo instead of his eyes, and that was a lucky break for me. It allowed me to set myself up fairly close in behind him and to be able to keep him in a direct line between Dog-Nose and me. That way I could pretty much sight down his rifle and figure where he was aiming.

Dog-Nose and Mrs. W____, meanwhile, were settled down in a thick stand of birches that bordered an even thicker stand of alder that bordered the marshy end of a small lake. It was a place where I and Dog-Nose had found a shitload (for literal) of moose sign in the past, and where we had been successful at jumping good bulls in past seasons. The lady was again proving herself to being a serious hunter by the mere fact that she and Dog-Nose were sitting dead still on their stand and not doing what I fully expected to find them doing. Me and W____ were just above them and about a hundred yards back on a low ridge in dense brush. Now I just had to wait for the gent to make his move.

W____ took off his headphones and laid them on the ground, switching off the radio. He picked up my gun and checked to see that there was a round in the chamber, and it was at this point that I realized I had been following this crackpot through all that impossible terrain while he had a round in the chamber and the safety was off. He could have just as easily shot *himself* with my gun. By the time the police got finished with that one, the brambles we had been pushing through would have been easier to untangle than what this murder case would look like.

Anyway, he puts the rifle up to his shoulder with his cheek a mile off the stock, and I can see I have got nothing to worry about on account of he does not know how to shoot and

he is aiming way wide of both Dog-Nose and his wife. So I figure on letting him go ahead and shoot. Either he is going to lay
himself flat out from the kick of that stock against his jaw, or I
will rush him and cold-cock him myself with the butt of my
spare rifle. Thank God it was going to be that simple.

The whole time I was following this fruitcake, I was
wondering just what I was going to do when the shit hit the
fan, as it were. I figured that if I conked him before he got a
shot off, I was leaving myself open to some serious legal problems. I mean, what if the guy later claimed as how he was in no
way up to anything like what we had figured and that everything I claimed turned out to look pretty thin and circumstan-
tial in the cold light of court many months after the fact? After
all, our case was less than air tight, based, as it was, solely on
the gut feelings of Dog-Nose and yours truly. So I decided that
unless I saw that his aim was dead on, I would let him go ahead
and fire and let the situation unfold however it would. I still do
not know what I would have done if I saw that his aim was true.
But that is now a mute point, as they say.

Anyway, he fires, and the shot is wide (though not
nearly as wide as I figured it to be on account of the wild jolt
he gives the gun when he yanks the trigger) and the bullet
thwaps into one of the birch trunks just about a foot to the left
of Mrs. W____. What happened next takes ten times as long to
tell as to happen.

I had risen to my feet and am lurching toward W____ in

the intention of knocking him down and grabbing my gun away before he can slam another round into the chamber and fire again. At the same time, looking just like a slow-motion movie, I see Dog-Nose and Mrs. W____ react to the bullet hitting the tree next to them as they look over at the birch, and then almost immediately they both swing their heads back to react to the crack of the rifle that came just a bit later on account of the distance. All the while, I see Mrs. W____'s mouth open and her own rifle barrel swing around in our direction, and just before I am about to reach W____, her scream and the sound of a shot reach me at the same time as the back of W____'s head blows out. He falls flat down on his back at my feet, and I see the single, perfect, clean little hole right in the middle of his forehead like a third eye, all three wide open and staring off to Heaven.

***

At the trial, I testified as how the whole thing was an accident. I suppose it had to be. There was no way that a person could hit a target as small as a man's forehead at a hundred yards by spinning around and one-handing a rifle without even aiming. I said as how it had to be just an incredible stroke of bad luck and that the woman's gun had just gone off accidentally when she jumped from hearing the husband's shot. The jury saw it that way, too, as you probably know if you were following the trial at the time. Still, though, I could never get rid of the feeling that, impossible as it seemed, Mrs. W____ got away with murder. Premeditated.

Dog-Nose, himself, always remained particularly tight-lipped about the whole business. It was as if he, too, suspected there was more to the whole thing than just the hand of Luck. At the trial, he pretty much just gave the facts, answering the lawyers' questions with uncharacteristic brevity. When he was asked his opinion of whether such a shot were possible intentionally, he only said, "It is my opinion that such a shot is one in several million, putting it, as far as I am concerned, in the realm of pure chance." And if we are to believe the newspapers, it was that statement that put the cork on the case. But although he never said so to me in so many words, I believe that Dog-Nose actually felt the lady was capable of pulling off the shot, not to mention a complex and devious scheme that precipitated the whole course of events. I expect we will never know. At least Dog-Nose won't.

***

As usual, I want to end this chapter with something from the box by Dog-Nose, and it seems to me that whatever that is ought to be somehow about women. Well, I have found something, all right, but I am hard put to figure out if this little ditty is about making love to a woman or playing a fish.

Knowing the Legend as I do, though, I would not be much surprised if that was exactly the kind of puzzle he meant it to be.
Here it is:

SONNET

She has, at last, engulfed my proffered lure,
And we have dallied long enough in fun;
Now time it is to spend her passion pure,
And blend our separate energies to one.
So, sensing that the final act is due,
Arched in thrashing ecstasies of zeal,
Letting up, now pressing hard, anew,
She lets me taste the heart of her appeal.
Now closing in, now moving off again;
Soon fury spends itself to loll serene.
I lift her close and sigh a soft "Amen,"
And tell her she's the best I've ever seen.
        And, once again, this fair and tasty dish
        Will leave my mustache redolent of fish.

7
MORE WOMEN

And everybody's sayin' that there's nobody meaner…

— Jan & Dean

I expect that after reading the last chapter, which is titled "Women," you will naturally figure this chapter, which is titled "More Women" to be some more exciting tales of Dog-Nose's loves and exploits with beautiful movie stars and rich wives, but I have fooled you. This chapter will be about a female person, all right, but not as you expect.

In my rummagings around in the box, I have come across quite a bit of stuff, some of which you have been reading. And one of the things is a story that Dog-Nose wrote about his granny. I know that on account of it is titled "Granny" and if that is not a dead giveaway I do not know what is. I also know that it is not just a made up story on account of how Dog-Nose has talked of this person on occasion throughout our partnership, and I do definitely recognize her as the person that Dog-Nose here refers to as his granny. So you can take my word for its authenticity as far as that goes. And here it is:

GRANNY

My maternal grandmother was one of the greatest one-armed carp fishermen who ever lived. According to Granny, the handicap was alternately attributable to "a shark attack in the South Pacific," "a pistol duel from which I emerged victorious," "frostbite suffered during an Arctic expedition," "a gangrenous condition brought on by a spider bite received while exploring the Amazon Basin," and "an imbroglio with drooling white slavers in the Middle East." I am reasonably certain the woman never set foot out of New England; nonetheless, at the time of their telling, most of those explanations were accepted hook, line, and sinker not only by me but by every one of my preadolescent compatriots. That all of those expository mishaps resulted in the loss of only *one* limb made her all the more venerable.

She, and I by association, were uncontested celebrities amongst my peers. They, however, without exception, were warned by their parents to stay clear of the old lady, who was widely regarded as being somewhat out of plumb. Consanguinity notwithstanding, I, too, was similarly advised, and not so much by my friends' parents as by my own.

Granny chose carp fishing by default. It is one of the few modes of fishing that a person with the dual handicaps of age and one-armedness can handle reasonably well alone. It is a sedentary form of angling requiring, more often than not, only a half-dozen casts a day. Live bait is unnecessary, and there is not the very frequent catching and unhooking of fish as occurs when angling for bluegills and perch. Fly casting was, of course, out of the question, though her knowledge of trout and their insect prey far exceeded that of anyone else I have ever met astream or aschool.

She had had a rod-holder bolted to an ancient, wooden, folding deck-chair, which held the rod at the proper, slightly forward angle for reeling, but which swivelled backward to allow for hook-setting. Attached to the chair, also, were a variety of hooks and clasps. They served no purpose once the chair was unfolded and occupied, but while folded, all her miscellaneous gear could be hung upon the chair, and the entire collection of paraphernalia could be carried with one arm. To me, she appeared the paragon of self-sufficiency. To anyone beyond the age of twelve, seeing her marching across the meadow with her portable fishing camp, she fit most classic descriptions of a certifiable psycho.

Her haunt was but one: The Meeting of the Waters, a site sacred to the aborigines, where the Sudbury and Assabet rivers join to form the Concord. There, on a bare and gently curving bank of mud and grass across from Egg Rock, Granny set up her daily camp in the shade of willows, a short stroll through meadows and woods from home.

Early in my life she had a dog, a large, malignant beast of heterogeneous bloodlines that accompanied her on her fishing expe-ditions and spent most of its wretched time wandering along the bank, wading in the benthic ooze, and rolling upon and then eating the washed-up corpses of riverine fauna. I suspected that the animal had been trained by the old lady to greet me upon my arrival at the river each day by hitting me in the chest with its forepaws, knocking me to the ground, and licking my entire face with its gore-fed tongue until I gagged from the stench of its breath and fur.

"Can't you stop that fetid carrion-eater from terrorizing me?" I begged the old lady continually.

"What are you, some kind of a spineless, little wimp?" was her standard reply. "Make him stop it yourself. Knock him down. Show him who's boss. Sock him in the snoot."

She knew I would do none of those things. The dog outweighed me nearly two to one. And, in some respects, I suppose I was some kind of spineless, little wimp. After all, I valued my young life above all else at that tender age, and even the relatively optimistic prospect of merely bearing disfiguring scars into my adolescence and beyond was enough to dissuade me from going hand-to-hand with the disgusting creature. It seemed equally clear to me, however, that disgorging my meals on a daily basis might also seriously impede my progress towards maturity. Something had to be done, and it apparently had to be done through intelligence rather than through either brawn or diplomacy. I filled a squeeze-bottle with a mixture of Tabasco sauce, chili powder, and cayenne pepper, and when the beast fell upon me in its customary greeting, I let him have it in the mouth and up both nostrils. The dog despised me after that but never came near me again, and Granny beat me to within an inch of my life while I considered the prospect of bearing disfiguring scars into my adolescence and beyond, assuming I made it that far. The old lady, I was beginning to realize, might well be as many bricks shy of a load as folks thereabouts had been intimating for as long as I could remember.

One perfect afternoon in my twelfth New England June, I crept through the ferns by the river with a week of school to go until I could look forward to another failed attempt by my parents to keep me out from under Granny's summer influence by exiling me to a camp in Maine that, as far as I could discern from its brochure, was far too long on the crafts of braiding plastic strips into keychains and punching holes in leather, and far too short on the arts of tying feathers and furs into insects and fooling the fins off trout. The attempt to send me to that place had been made and thwarted two years running, and I had no reason to assume that this summer would not follow a similar pattern. The thwarting was accomplished by the old lady's padlocking me in a steamer trunk in her closet until my parents agreed to forget the whole idea, and although the trunk would now be a good deal less comfortable due to my significant growth over the past year, I was still somewhat willing to brave the ordeal once again. Summers had become a good deal more tolerable since the dog had been shot by an irate breeder of champion Irish setters whose bitches had all been debauched by the brute.

I emerged from the woods and stood by the ancient bole of the willow in whose shade, some ten yards down the bank, Granny sat in her deck chair, her back to me, unaware of my presence. Out on the brown, slow current, another ten yards, bobbed the green and red, wooden float from which Granny hung her potato slice with the embedded, needle-sharp, number two hook. I saw the float bounce once, and then heard Granny, whom I had thought to be asleep, begin her customary chant.

"Bobber bobbin'. Bobber bobbin'. Bobber bobbin'. Bobber bobbin'. Bobber bobbin'. Bobber bobbin'. Bobber under. Bobber under. Bobber under. Bobber under. Bobber under. Bobber under. Bobber down! Bobber down! Wham!" as she yanked back on the rod as though throwing a Porsche into second gear.

And I could hear the drag whine all the way back where I stood, and the rod bowed and pulsed as the black line headed out into deep water, Granny whooping and slapping her hat on her knees, mashing it back on her head as the crazy line slowed for a moment, and she grabbed the handle on the reel and wound furiously, trying to regain some line. But I heard the whir of drag as she cranked, and I knew that nothing had been taken in...more line whining out as Granny now held on to the rod butt, and suddenly the chair was moving...Granny digging her heels into the hard mud bank as strange sets of drag-marks from the chair and her feet appeared behind her on the bank... Granny picking up speed and reaching the water's edge as I, frozen by the amazing sight of it all, finally thawed and ran to her aid, jumping into the river ahead of her and turning like a tight-end pivoting to receive a pass, and taking the full brunt of her and the chair against my shins, digging my feet into the sandy bottom, which was softer than I had imagined, sinking down into quicksand while the fish still pulled, with amazing force, the chair and Granny against my arms and knees. Granny, white-knuckled, holding the rod, now lets go...has me by the throat...I, falling backwards, feet solidly embedded in the bottom muck, while the chair rides up the front of my body and cracks me in the chin with an explosion that echoes down the river. Under I go, the weight of Granny and the chair upon my chest as I feel myself dying there, trying to save the old lady from a killer carp.

I awoke from a dream of doggy death-breath, shivering in the hot sun, lying on the muddy bank while Granny alternately pressed upon my chest with her hand and slapped me across the face with her hat, unable to do both at once, thank God.

"What happened?" I asked.

"Damn line broke," said Granny. "Didn't you hear the report? Sounded like a rifle shot."

"I thought that was my jaw breaking," I said, wiggling my chin side to side with my hand.

"Your jaw's fine," Granny assured me after inflicting her exploratory probing upon my entire head and neck. "That must have been some fish, hey, boy? I'm still on the fence as to whether I should be grateful to you for your gallantry or knock the living piss out of you for making me lose it."

"What do you mean?" I asked incredulously. "Do you actually doubt that you'd by now be as drowned as a fished-out nightcrawler if I hadn't helped? Do you really think, on the other hand, that you might've landed that fish?"

"It's well within the realm of probability," she said sitting on my chest and glowering, punctuating every third word with a stab of her finger to my sternum. "Why shouldn't that chair float? It's made of wood. I might have followed that carp downriver a distance and wore him out. What's so farfetched? Hey, sonny?"

I rolled her off me and jumped up filled with the righteous indignation one feels, particularly at the age of twelve, when one's obvious heroism is downplayed by one's unglued grandmother whom one has just saved from certain death. "That chair would have sunk like a rock, dragged you under, flipped over, cracked you on the back of the head somewhere out in mid-channel, and you'd have been found, days later, washed against the pilings of the Old North Bridge. That's what would've happened. But you, on the other hand, prefer to believe that you might have water-skied on your behind, under the bridge, pulled by the monster until, somewhere beyond the Great Meadows probably, (am I getting this right?), you wore it down to the point where it lost its mind and grounded itself like a pilot whale, allowing you to reel yourself up onto shore after it."

"Something like that," she said, standing up and brushing herself off.

"The fact is," I pressed further, trying to get her goat, "that you're too stubborn to admit that I really did save your life. You, on the other hand, would rather believe that I cost you a trophy carp. You, on the other hand, would like me to believe that you'd rather I'd let you drown." Her eyes now blazing, Granny threw her weight into the punch, swinging with her lonely right fist as she caught me across the left side of my abused jaw. Stars and planets burst behind my closed eyelids as I went down again on the muddy bank, and just before losing consciousness for the second time in ten minutes, I heard the confirmation that my teasing had not escaped the old lady. Granny standing over me, her finger flailing like a bullwhip, bellowed, "And stop referring to me as 'on the other hand', you perverse little s.o.b."

****

As I said earlier, this woman who Dog-Nose has here written about did actually exist and was his real granny. On the afternoon of December 20, 1968, just outside of Concord, New Hampshire, Mildred Standish Coleridge, the lady in question, was involved in a near fatal traffic accident that resulted in the loss of her right leg.

She was on her way to do some last-minute Christmas shopping at a brand new shopping center called Head of the Sphinx Mall, which had just opened that week to a great deal of hoop-de-doo and publicity. The poor woman, who had enough trouble driving what with her having but the one arm and being none too quick in the reflexes at that age, was just pulling into the entrance of the place when she was hit squarely broadside and flipped over by one of several ambulances that was leaving the place at about a hundred miles an hour. Just before she arrived, there had been a disastrous explosion that took out most of the new shops, injuring and killing untold numbers of Christmas shoppers and storeowners for, as you can imagine what with Christmas just around the bend plus the gala grand opening to boot, the place was about as packed full as a bank giving away free samples.

Luckily for granny, the lost leg was on the same side as the good arm, so she could tuck a crutch under there and still get around some. I hear the tragedy pretty much soured her even on carp fishing, though, and she does not do much of that anymore.

8
MEYER THE TYER

Everybody knows the secret.
Everybody knows the score.
I have finally found a place to live,
In the presence of the Lord.

— Blind Faith

I suppose it is the same with most of your so-called service professions where you spend most of your time dealing
with the public. You meet a lot of what you might call your
eccentrics. I do not know if the guiding business attracts more
than its share of weirdos, but it seems like it might. Maybe it is
simply that the guiding business caters more to the rich, and
that it is just rich people who are stranger than most. That has
strong possibilities.

Naturally, you meet a lot of people who are memorable for their good personalities, too, but they do not stick out so much or so long. It is definitely the ones playing with the shortest decks that hang in your memory. I have already told of the couples with connubial tribulations. They were common and do not distinguish themselves from the crowd, except for those that developed into dangerous situations like the ones I have written about.

But there was one character that was an eye-opener above all others and had nothing to do with marriage or wealth or anything else of that sort. He was a one-of-a-kind oddball that I never quite could figure out what to make of, though Dog-Nose took to him almost right away. For my taste, he was more dangerous than any of the others. He was not out to cheat you in the weasely way of Sonny Lematina, nor was he out to shoot you like any of those crazy husbands and wives. In fact there was nothing physical he was likely or even capable of doing to you. It was his way of thinking that was so alarming. But I should explain who this fellow was and how we happened to meet him.

It was back when things were really starting to pick up. You might say it was just about when Dog-Nose's popularity and legendary status was reaching its crest that we got a letter from one Meyer Fleigel, better known as Meyer the Tyer, who was himself something of a legend in his own time. It was not uncommon, back then, to be getting letters from the rich and famous. During those days, I and Dog-Nose guided presidents, writers, artists, luminaries of one sort or another, and what you call your captains of industry. The worst type, which we were called upon to host at a fairly regular frequency, was the so-called outdoor celebrity type. This is your fellow who either writes a regular and well-read column in one of the big outdoor magazines or has a radio or television show on the subject or authors a batch of books or whatever. It is this type who usually thinks he knows more than you do, even though he has never set foot in your particular bailiwick before in his life. He will come up after having spent some time chasing tarpon or bonefish on the saltwater flats of Florida or South America or someplace and then claim that he knows all about catching Atlantic salmon on account of his vast experience with fish that are as about as similar to salmon as a penguin is to a grouse.

But we put up with that sort for the publicity we got out of them, and some of them turned out to be okay in spite of themselves. A few of this type came into the outdoor field from the side door, as it were. They were the ones who made fishing tackle or guns or clothing or related things for the sportsmen, and many of them were only too eager to give away free samples to the likes of the Legend. Those fellows were the easiest to get along with, for although they were well travelled and experienced in hunting and fishing on account of they could write off all their trips as business expenses, they were also regular people with a business to run and a fair understanding of public relations. And although Dog-Nose had a strict policy of never doing commercial endorsements of products, it could be worth a couple of arms, legs, and other bodily parts to a manufacturer to have Dog-Nose just using your product so as other sports could see it. That made those fellows nicer to deal with on account of their wanting to do nothing that would get us pissed off at them. But I think many of them would have been genuinely decent sorts anyway.

But getting back to Meyer the Tyer, you have undoubtedly heard of him if you are any kind of serious fly fisherman. His salmon and trout flies are collected in the Museum of Flyfishing down in Vermont along with the likes of Carrie Stevens, the Darbees, Theodore Gordon, and the rest. He was as famous as any of them and had, for fifteen years running, tied the fly that caught the first salmon of the year out of Bangor Pool on the Penobscot, which was traditionally presented to the president of the United States (the salmon, not the fly) as an annual ceremony. That is a remarkable thing in anybody's book, for there are many different anglers responsible for the catching of those fifteen salmon over those years, and every one of them happened to be using one of Meyer's flies. That is how legendary he was.

Actually, about six of those fifteen fish were caught by the same fellow, one Salmo Sam, who used to live down by the Bangor Pool in a hollow log during the first few weeks of each season until the spring of '66 when the river flooded more than usual and swept the log out to sea with Sam inside it dead drunk. A Nova Scotia-bound ferry, headed up the Bay of Fundy, picked up the log about a month later with Sam drowned inside. Apparently the punky wood swelled up when it got wet and held Sam like one of those Chinese finger traps. That put a quick end to Sam's six-year run of catching the presidential salmon, all with flies tied by Meyer the Tyer.

So that was the caliber of Meyer's renown by the time he wrote to us about taking him out trout fishing in the upper Kennebec region. The request meant not a pile of rabbit raisins to me but for the fact that yet another celebrity prima donna was about to saddle us with his adolescent behavior. But Dog-Nose was as excited about the visit as a teenager in a whorehouse.

"Junior," he says to me, "you are about to meet a man who is like no one you have met before. I've read about this fellow and have looked forward to meeting him with great enthusiasm. I'll be interested to see your reaction to him."

"What makes this guy so hot?" I ask him. "I ain't seen you so excited about guiding anybody since that famous nymphomaniac Italian countess showed up."

"This is different," he says. "This man is not only a master of the fly-tyer's art; he is a world-class scholar as well. This unassuming immigrant, who ekes out his meager living in the millinery trade and ties exquisite flies for the sporting trade, is also an intellectual who writes wonderfully erudite works of philosophy."

"For the thinking trade?" I ask.

"It's just that we so rarely get to guide someone who has something to say about anything besides himself," says Dog-Nose with a look that could wither an anti-intellectual.

"Okay," I say, "I'll reserve comment until I meet this character."

Holy smokes! Dog-Nose was right. Meyer the Tyer was not like anybody I had ever met before. Here was an old fellow of about seventy-five years, dressed like he stepped out of those brown photographs from the 1890s. He wore black baggy pants and a black suit jacket over a white shirt, and on his head was a wide-brimmed black hat about as flat and styleless as a serving tray. For a hat-maker, you would think he could do a little better for himself. Pouring out from under the hat, which I never saw him take off his head once during the ten days he was with us, was a mop of stringy gray curls that hung down the side of his head like filamentous algae. And on his face grew a mustache and beard that would make the inside of a mattress look orderly and well-groomed. That is how he showed up for a fishing trip in the Maine woods. And that is what he wore for the whole ten days, except for the waders that we provided him. On top of all this, he spoke with an accent that you could not cut with a well-honed filleting knife.

"Za plesha to mit chew," he says to me, shaking my hand upon arriving, and I honestly did not know he was speaking English at the time. Although I would love to be able to imitate his speech with the written word, as it were, it would take me forever to write it and you even longer to read it. So from now on I will write what he said in regular English except where it makes sense to do otherwise, as when he utters his favorite profanity, "fockink scombeg," which was quite often.

It turns out, as I gathered over the period of his stay with us, that this fellow had been a Hasidic Jew (a religious order I am still not too clear on, especially since Dog-Nose kept assuring me that Meyer's singular theology had evolved into something having little resemblance to any known religion) from somewhere in eastern Europe who came to this country as a child and took up the family trade of hat-making. Back then, ladies' hats were big on feathers, and Meyer always had a supply of scraps and leftovers. Once, while wandering around midtown Manhattan, he saw some salmon flies in the window of a fishing shop and was taken by their beauty and the realization that here was a way to make some extra money from all the feather scraps he had around. So he talked the owner into teaching him some fly-tying techniques and began to supply the shop with flies, never really understanding what they were used for. Finally he got the shop owner to take him along to one of the famous Catskill streams and show him how the flies were used. Of course, there are no salmon in those waters, but the owner showed him how to fish trout flies and how the salmon flies that Meyer had been tying acted in the water. Understanding that, finally, Meyer began to tie better salmon flies and eventually expanded into trout flies, too. Before long, his flies were among the most sought after in the country.

All of that biographical background was told to us by Meyer during his stay. And I think I have gotten most of it right, although listening to him talk was a lot like having a conversation with another angler while you are both fishing an area of noisy, fast water and standing about fifteen yards from each other. You can hear the voices but you only actually get about every third or fourth word. So when you're finished yelling back and forth, you have got the general gist of the exchange, but the details have all been washed downstream.

"So vot de fock shoot I know abot fishink?" he would say, and I would have to not only translate that into something understandable, but then decide whether he really expected me to answer the question or not. I have never heard a man ask so many so-called rhetorical questions in all my life.

In any case, the above question was intended by Meyer to illustrate the fact that although he was one of the most celebrated fly tyers who ever lived, he did not necessarily have much aptitude at the intended use of his creations, namely fly fishing.

"I have had such tribulations in my attempts at fly fishing," says Meyer in his gargly, throat-clearing accent. "So, like the trials of Job, why should it not lead me to a deep and unswerving belief in the Almighty at a time when I was beginning to lose faith?"

"You, a devoutly religious man, were losing faith in

God?" asks Dog-Nose, getting into the question-asking mode himself, so that whole conversations began to sound like a quiz or a game show but with hardly anybody ever actually coming up with an answer.

"So what's so astonishing?" says Meyer. "Have not even the most pious throughout history suffered moments of doubts? What, one's faith should not waver when one hears of innocents dying, children starving, injustices being freely and routinely committed by ruthless and greedy fockink scombegs all over the world?"

(Just to make sure you can fully appreciate the difficulty involved in my having to translate all this for you, that last bit would have sounded something like "rootless ant griddy fockink scombegs aluffa de voilt.")

"And you're saying that your faith was restored as a result of fly fishing?" asks Dog-Nose.

"Sure, why not?" says Meyer. "That and other things."

"What do you mean?" asks Dog-Nose, finally asking a question that has some sense to it.

"What I mean," says Meyer as we both lean forward to catch this great crumb of wisdom like two guys trying to take off their pants while sitting down, "is that can one honestly believe it is possible for the world to be so screwed up without Divine intervention? Can purely random events so consistently produce such predictably focked up results? For Christ's sake, there *has* to be a God to make such a mess, don't you see it?"

Dog-Nose and me both sit bolt upright like we have been goosed and stare at each other and then back at Meyer. Meyer, meanwhile, pausing for dramatic effect, pours himself a shot of Scotch, picks a blackfly off the surface of the amber liquid, and guides the rim of the glass up inside the tangle of whiskers hanging around his mouth.

"What are you saying?" asks Dog-Nose.

"Nothing new," says Meyer. "Throughout the Bible, God is characterized as a vengeful, wrathful, all-powerful deity. Since the beginnings of Judaism, have Jews been worshipping God because He is just, or because He is merciful, or because He is loving, or has a good sense of humor, or is competent at doing his job in the least? No, for crying out loud. We worship God because He will bust our asses if we do not cower before him and make him feel important. He is one powerful sunemabitch."

"Holy shit," I finally blurt out and grab for the bottle, "that's outright blasphemous to talk about God the way you just did."

"You think so?" says Meyer after I just told him in no uncertain terms that I thought so. "You think I blaspheme when I acknowledge out here in the woods, naked in the full presence of God, that he is powerful and can squash me just as I squash one of these fockink scombeg blackflies that are eating me alive out here?" Meyer's arms are flailing around like a tipped-over helicopter gone berserk. "Why should you not believe that I am worshipping him by saying that? Why not consider that he is most appeased when we rail against him, thus confirming his awesome power?"

Dog-Nose has a look on his face like he has just undressed the most beautiful woman of his life and she has turned out to be not only a mannequin, but a male one at that.

"You think you know God?" continues Meyer, slathering himself with some kind of horribly stinky, jellied bug dope that he has scooped out of an ancient Krank's shaving cream jar. "Let me tell you about Him. You know those big, fat, sadistic, southern sheriffs with the mirrored sunglasses and the bellies hanging over their pants? That is what God looks like, my friend. And that is what God *is* like. He is just like those sadistic bestids with an adolescent, toilet sense of humor. Am I not right?"

You have got to picture this scene. The three of us are camped next to a river that is running silky-smooth and soundless except for the occasional *plip* of a rising trout. It is late in the afternoon of a warm summer day, and the birds have begun to pick up their evening chorus. Blackflies are hovering around us as they are nearly always up here, and we are all sitting on camp chairs outside the tents in a clearing beneath towering evergreens. Except for the annoyance of the flies, which you can lessen considerably by applying some decent repellent, the place is a paradise on Earth, as peaceful as you could ever hope to find. And here is this hairy blasphemer in his black, rumpled suit and white shirt, calling down the wrath of God upon us all.

131

I do not know about how Dog-Nose was taking it, but I personally was fully expecting Mt. Katahdin, looming in the northeast, to erupt and send fire and brimstone down upon the heads of us lousy sinners and a tidal wave of mud and ash to come pouring down the river to bury us in an eternal tomb of concrete.

"You see these gotdem blackflies?" continues Meyer, finally asking a question that I have no trouble determining as purely rhetorical. "Why is it not reasonable to believe that God has sent these to us to show that He is not angry with my attitude? Do you believe that if He were truly angry He could not, in all His power, summon up a plague worse than these crappy little flies? To believe that God is that impotent would truly be blasphemous, would it not? But He is not angry; He is happy. He is having a good laugh at our expense by sending these focking pests to bother us. That is His focking childish sense of humor."

"That's certainly an interesting theory," says Dog-Nose, stretching his legs and smashing a blackfly on the side of his head.

"Theory shmeory," says Meyer. "Did you ever notice how every time you settle down to some important task, you have to pee? You have to stop what you are doing just as you finally reach the most crucial point of accomplishment or at the precise time when it is most disastrous to let yourself be torn from the complexity at hand. Just at that moment when you are most precariously holding the ends of fifty-dozen tiny threads, either physically or mentally, that will absolutely tangle themselves into chaos if you let them go, you have to go pee. And is it not also true that if you are waiting for an important phone call, no matter how long you postpone the inevitable, the call will finally come when you are on the toilet? Yet you think this is chance? This is God, my friend. This is his focking, sadistic, adolescent, toilet sense of humor. May I show you something?"

Without waiting for an answer, because of course the question had been rhetorical again, Meyer stood up and began to put on a pair of hip boots that were hanging from the branch of a spruce.

"Notice, my friends, how the water is like a beautiful mirror?" he says, lifting his chin toward the river in a gesture of pointing while his hands were busy with the boots. "And do you not see the tops of the trees, how still they are as if awaiting the word of God? There is not a breath of air moving, not the slightest zephyr, am I correct?"

We shook our heads in agreement, I and Dog-Nose, as we watched the now-booted Meyer, still wearing the black suit and wide-brimmed hat, begin to rig his fly rod. As carefully as though threading a needle, he worked the leader up through the guides one by one, and although I could not see how it was possible, the line seemed to constantly slip from his steady fingers and fall back down through the guides so that he had to start all over again about six times until my insides started to feel like somebody was whitewater canoeing in them and I took the rod from Meyer and threaded it myself without any further ado. He thanked me with what you might call your enigmatic smile on his face and took the rod.

"How is the wind?" he asks.

I and Dog-Nose tear our eyes from his and look around. Still nothing stirred. The world was not breathing, just like us.

"What fly do you recommend, my friend?" he says to Dog-Nose. And Dog-Nose says that since there is not much of anything going on out there, something generic like an Adams or Royal Coachman ought to be as good as anything. So Meyer digs a battered flybox out of his gear and opens it and takes out a #16 Adams and holds it up to Dog-Nose. "Fine," says Dog-Nose, and as Meyer is tying it onto his leader, he momentarily looks up at us and gestures with his head and eyes that we should once again check the surroundings. The trees are dead still, the water flows unruffled. Meyer applies some floatant to his Adams and steps to the edge of the water. He glances again at the tops of the trees, and our own eyes follow. Even the little flimsy tiptops of the hemlocks, as responsive to wind as feathers, are lying limp and still.

Meyer steps into the river to within a foot of his wader-tops and begins false casting upstream. There is the slurping rise of a large trout within an easy thirty-foot cast. Meyer sends the fly into the final backcast and brings it forward in a perfectly beautiful, tight loop headed right for the spot above the rise and suddenly, all hell breaks loose. A squall line comes down the river out of nowhere, bending the trees into wildly thrashing parodies of fishing rods fighting monster trout. The water in the glassy run has turned into heavy rapids from the wind, and Meyer's line, having never reached its target, is stretched straight out behind him in the gale. Then, just as suddenly, it is calm again.

Meyer comes sloshing out of the river, soaking wet. "You see the wonderful sense of humor?" he says. He leans the rod against a tree where it immediately falls on the ground, and after bending down to pick it back up and picking up his overturned chair, which blew over in the wind, he sits down and pours himself another shot of Scotch. I and Dog-Nose are speechless. The rod, for no apparent reason, slides across the rough trunk of the hemlock as though it is as smooth as a birch and clatters to the ground again. Meyer just smiles.

The next morning, there is a ferocious mayfly hatch on the river and the water is boiling with rising trout. We all of us don chest waders so as to get right out into the best spots and not be limited by the height of hippers. Again I am moved by a frustrated churning in my gut to help Meyer rig up his rod on account of the way he keeps dropping the line down all the guides after almost getting it to the top. How in hell he ever gets any flies tied is beyond me.

Dog-Nose positions Meyer out in the run and proceeds to instruct him on the best procedure for working the risers in his immediate area. Meyer works out a few yards of line. Out in the middle of the run, there is a slight breeze, though nothing to inhibit short-distance casts. I watch as Meyer false casts and snags his backcast in a tiny, dead twig about twelve feet above the water that I did not even notice protruding out from one of the bankside trees. It is the only thing within twenty yards that could possibly interrupt the flight of his line, and he found it.

The fly has embedded itself in the twig well enough so that it cannot be shaken out, and Meyer has to snap the leader and tie on another fly. He dismisses Dog-Nose's offer to tie on the new fly for him.

"What? You should pay for my misfortune?" Meyer says to Dog-Nose. "No, my friend, you go ahead and cast. Show me that these fish can be caught."

So, while Meyer ties on a new fly, Dog-Nose goes to work shooting perfect loops over eager fish and landing four fat brookies before Meyer is ready to try again. It is something beautiful to behold. Even Meyer stops to watch the Legend at work and gives him a hearty round of sincere applause as the last trout is netted.

"Your turn," says Dog-Nose to Meyer.

"I should be so lucky," says Meyer and begins to work his line out again. Just as he sends his cast forward, the fly hits his rod tip and ties itself there with about six inches of tippet. The rest of the line slaps down in front of him and drifts back with the current, tangling around his legs. "Ah," he says,

"God's in his heaven; all's right with the world."

Undaunted, he untangles everything and tries again. This time, his backcast dips slightly, and the fly touches the water behind him, coming up hooked to a small leaf that holds his forward cast up in the breeze, luffing and buzzing, and the whole loop of line collapses and lands in a pile on his head.

"You fockink scombeg," shrieks Meyer, trembling and livid, the line draping down over his hat and shoulders like a prayer shawl, his rod-holding fist shaking at the heavens. "You pig-eating drek."

"Whoa, there," I finally say, rattled by the profanity of this outburst, "it's one thing to call God a son of a bitch like you did last night, but don't you think this is going too far?"

Meyer looks at me like I am five years old and he is my grandfather and my mother just died. His eyes are filled with pity for the lack of understanding that are in mine. And he is deeply moved by my innocence.

"You do not understand what I have been saying, do you, my friend?" he says, lifting the flyline off his hat and letting it drop to the water, then putting his arm around my shoulder. "It is the passion and manner of my worship that upsets you."

"I ain't never in my life heard of anybody worshipping God by calling Him a scumbag," I say.

"Yet is it not, in fact, truly worship to so fervently acknowledge the power of God?" says Meyer. "What do you think worship is, anyway? You wince at my language. Yet who has ever said that God requires our good wishes or our compliments? No, my friend, God only requires our fear, our obedience, our devotion, and our confirmation of His horrible omnipotence. And what better way is there of appeasing Him than to show Him how much He has hurt us. He loves it. The more foul and violent my rages become the more passionate is my worship, and He knows it. If He were angry with me, He could truly punish me, but this is merely an expression of His divine sense of humor, and my lot is to provide His amusement."

"But are you not taught in Deuteronomy, Chapter VI, verse 5 that you are to 'love the Lord thy God with all thy heart, and with all thy soul, and with all thy might?'" says Dog-Nose.

"What are you, a rabbi?" says Meyer. "So when have I said I do not love the Lord? You think that just because I scream nasty things at Him that I do not love Him? He is the Lord, for heaven's sake. I *have* to love Him. He constantly does rotten things to me, but do you think for a minute He does not love me? He is the Lord. He loves every one of us. What you say to Him has nothing to do with anything. It is that you say it with conviction to the depth of your soul that matters."

With this, Dog-Nose, who had been listening with trout rising all around him and bumping his legs, says: "There is, in all this, Meyer, an appealing logic to your theology. But how do you know that God actually has anything to do with your failure to catch trout? How do you know you're not simply the world's worst flyfisherman simply by virtue of a pure lack of aptitude?"

Meyer smiles his patient smile and says, just as he did last night before the wind demonstration, "May I show you something?" And he proceeds to take the fly off the end of his tippet and put it in his jacket pocket. Then he signals us to step back and starts to work out some line. With fifty feet of line out, he is casting the most perfect loops I have ever seen, setting the empty end of his leader down precisely on the centers of the rings caused by the still-rising trout. He hits the centers of each ring, just before they start to elongate and droop downstream, as though he is Robin Hood or William Tell's Overture or somebody hitting a bulls-eye with an arrow. Then he lets out some more line and some more until the entire thirty yards of line is whistling back and forth in the air over his head with the precision and beauty of a stunt pilot flying a whole squadron of jets in formation, and he says, "Do you see that red maple leaf over by the bank? The one wiggling at the end of that little twig?" And me and Dog-Nose look and see that there is no mistaking which leaf he is talking about even though it is a hundred feet away.

Then Meyer, who has been keeping all that line working back and forth over his head in an unbelievable series of false casts, lets go with the forward cast of that whole length of line and the very tip of his leader snaps against that little red leaf and pops it off the twig like it was shot with a bullet. All in all, there was no denying that the man put on an exhibition of such casting precision and accuracy that it made Dog-Nose's earlier display look as clumsy and graceless as if it had been performed by a dancing bear.

Dog-Nose looked like he had been struck dumb for good, but then broke out of his trance and asked Meyer: "I don't get it. If God were really out to make you the butt, why didn't He screw up that long cast and make you look foolish?"

"If He did that," answered Meyer, "how would He ever make you realize I am right?"

A very strange feeling came over me at that point. It was like the feeling you get the first time you do something new, like start a new school or take on a new task that you are not sure you are any good at but that everybody else is depending on you to do right. There was something in Meyer's logic that made terrible sense. And that is what was so terrible.

We fished all the rest of the day and the rest of the week without Meyer making one single successful cast while a fly was on his line. And we watched him worship his God until the veins popped out on his neck and forehead, and his hands bled from punching them into the rocky banks, and his throat was raw from raging.

"The man is either a lunatic or a prophet," says Dog-Nose after Meyer's departure.

"What, he can't be both?" I answer.

Not long after this episode with Meyer Fleigel, we

learned that he had a new book published. It was titled, *He Loves You When You Swear*, and in it Meyer expounds on his peculiar theological beliefs. He sent us a copy, having marked a chapter in which he actually recounts some of the same occurrences I have related here.

The book eventually became something of a success. At least it attracted the attention of college students and was given the kinds of reviews that have a tendency to give movies, books, and other popular forms of art the status of what you call your cult followings.

He was even invited, on an increasingly regular basis, to bookstores throughout the Northeast to do so-called book signings. The last occurred at a bookstore called The Title Page, which had just opened in the Head of the Sphinx Mall outside of Concord, New Hampshire, where the owners of The Title Page had invited Meyer and a couple of other regional celebrities up as a promotion for the opening. The shop and most of the rest of the shopping center were obliterated by an explosion at 2:12 p.m., on the day of the signing, just before Christmas in 1968. It was thought that every one of the 37 people in the bookstore at the time of the explosion had been killed, but nine days after the catastrophe, as workmen cleared away the rubble, Meyer was found under the remains of the store's restroom, hungry, but without a scratch.

9
GREENWARS

But what's confusing you is just the nature of my game.

— The Rolling Stones

It was a real Dickens of a time. I mean by that that it was the kind of time Charles Dickens wrote about when he wrote those lines about the best of times and the worst of times and the age of wisdom and the age of Aquarius and light and darkness and all. And of course I am talking about the late 1960s when all hell broke loose to the point where even off in the backwoods of Maine you could not remain ignorant of it for long.

I and Dog-Nose were by that time beyond drafting age, and I was Canadian anyway, as I have said, so was not in much danger of suddenly being dragged off to the jungles. But that is not to say that the chaos of the age was not to touch us, for as I have tried to impress upon you throughout this book, the guiding business and the celebrity business were each magnets of the most powerful kind for attracting the oddest sorts and circumstances the way an outhouse draws flies. And we were involved in both.

Of course at that particular time, drugs played a large part in the weirdness we began to experience on a regular basis as rich, young, so-called flower people began coming up to the wilderness to feed their heads, as they said. There was one fellow who hired us to guide him up to the west branch of the Penobscot as I recall it, and every day all he did was to take some drug before breakfast and then go out into the river with all his clothes on and no waders. Holding his fly rod, on which he painstakingly tied a fly recommended by Dog-Nose, who he was careful to always ask for advice, he would walk out to a mid-stream boulder, sit down up to his neck in the water, lean his back against the rock, and stay like that all day. Then he would come back in to camp about supper time and tell us the most wonderful stories about all the trophy trout he had hallucinated catching that day. He had those fantasies down to such minute detail as to the nature of the hatches, the flies he had tried, the takes and refusals in a variety of lies, knots slipping and leaders breaking, sliding on slimy rocks, the sights and sounds of not only fighting fish but of birds and wind and his line swishing through the air, minks coming out onto streamside rocks to leave their droppings filled with the scales of young trout and the shells of crayfish, and just about every perception a fine angler and woodsman would have on a normal day of fishing, and then some.

We could not complain about the harshness of the work nor the beauty of his stories, which were ornamented with some of the most phantasmagorical and imaginative goings on that I have ever heard. And even Dog-Nose continually expressed delight in the images that the fellow related. Still, I never had the gumption to try any of the stuff when offered, although I am not too sure about Dog-Nose.

I recall a time shortly after one of those type left that Dog-Nose went off by himself to do some fishing during a day before a new sport was to show up, and he came back spouting a tale about meeting some gal along one of the pools. Now that may be of no great improbability where *you* normally fish. But up where we were camped, the likelihood of seeing another human being of any gender, but particularly female, was as good as meeting a whole major-league ball club in full uniform taking batting practice.

Naturally, according to Dog-Nose, the two of them ended up rolling in the shallows with their waders jammed down around their ankles and them joined together at the hip, but that sort of thing was not sufficient to lend neither credence nor qualms to the tale on account of the frequency with which those things really did happen to Dog-Nose.

What leads me to believe it to have been pure, drug-induced fantasy is the fact that he did not come back with any fish. Women or no women, it was a rare roll in the river, as it were, that left Dog-Nose fishless. So I believe the fact that he was drenched to his neck when he returned had less to do with "fishing for trout in some peculiar stream," as Mr. Shakespeare has once called what Dog-Nose claimed to be doing with the young lady, than with imbibing some of the stuff our young sport might have left behind.

Those acid-head sorts were mostly gentle and harmless and were not much trouble to take care of most of the time. There was, of course, a bad time or two when somebody had a faulty reaction to something and took to the idea that he was going to die. I remember one fellow who got that certainty into his head and flew into a serious panic of the screaming meemies variety. My reaction was simply to hand him a shovel and tell him to dig himself a decent grave so we would not have to haul his sorry ass all the way back to Boston or New York or wherever he was from, but Dog-Nose told me that that was not quite the right approach, and he talked the poor fellow through his crisis like a mother.

I had no patience for that sort of babysitting. I figured if a person were to get himself into a predicament by experimenting with so-called psychedelics, then it is his own problem to get out of it. When I have ever gotten myself shitfaced to the point of death on good old fashioned alcohol, I have never had anybody try to talk me out of puking my guts up and passing out on my face. Whatever happened to being responsible for your own actions?

Anyway, it is not really the drug-heads I was intending to complain about. It was the political activists that seemed to have sprung up like mushrooms in August during those days. Everybody who was not too stoned to move seemed to be shaking his fists at something. If it was not at the government, it was at the universities, or the industries, or the police, or the National Guard, or the landlord, or their parents, or the high cost of drugs. Everybody had a cause, and some of those people got dangerous.

The ones that had the most severe effect on us, especially on Dog-Nose, and in a way I think brought on the beginning of the end for us, was a bunch who called themselves APEs, which stood for the Alliance for the Preservation of the Environment. These were activists who were the hard-core militants, and they had gotten it into their heads that Dog-Nose was their so-called spiritual leader.

No doubt we all did share a love of the outdoors and had certain interests in common. Sorry little hunting and fishing is possible in a housing development or a shopping mall or a parking lot. Most folks will readily agree to that. But some who agree will simply shrug their shoulders, some will try to work through governments and lawyers and whatall to stop such things in a sane way, some will move off to places where such things are not going on, and others will go completely nuts.

I and Dog-Nose probably fit into a combination of the kinds who move away and those who work through laws, for while we felt relatively safe from interference in our remote areas where we normally guided, Dog-Nose was a letter writer of the most frenzied sort at times, sending off correspondences to congressmen and senators and magazines about the dangers of your so-called over-development and environmental abuse.

Dog-Nose was one of the most vocal voices at the time about what he called your habitat destruction, and he wrote many letters and longer articles explaining how over-development was not so much an aesthetic problem, but as how it had much longer-range ramifications by reducing the habitats of plants and animals to a point where they could no longer find food and breeding areas to support big enough populations that could continue themselves. He believed that this was not just an American problem but one that affected the whole world and would not be surprised if the cure for cancer had already been lost forever by having some unknown plant burned off the face of the Earth to make way for the herds of cows that supplied the fast-food hamburger joints from the jungles of South America.

Anyway, it was that kind of outspoken writing and radical thought that attracted outspoken radicals to Dog-Nose's side. First he was a national legend, and then he was a national legend with a message. It was no wonder that the APEs took to him like leaches to a snapping turtle. Unfortunately, those people were not your basic bird-watcher types.

The Alliance for the Preservation of the Environment was a bunch that had managed to get itself right up near the top of the FBI's list of most dangerous organizations, although at the time, it seems like even the Girl Scouts were up there someplace, what with so many political groups being targeted by government paranoia. But the APEs were right up there with the Simian Liberation Army, or whatever it was, and the Black Panthers and all the rest of the militant menagerie. In fact, the APEs called themselves "environmental terrorists" and had the press to prove it. But let me back up a minute.

Dog-Nose was not your violent sort. In fact, when that slogan came out about making love and not war, Dog-Nose latched onto the idea of having it tattooed down the length of the most vital part of his anatomy during one drunken evening on Moosehead. And if it were not for the fact that it was a good two hundred miles of bad roads to the nearest tattoo parlor, he might well have done it.

My point is, though, that Dog-Nose was as far from militant as the sun is from Seattle, but in one of his letters to some magazine or other, he once suggested the possibility of your so-called civil disobedience for stopping some of the most destructive kinds of development. By that he pretty much meant nothing more radical than sitting down in front of bulldozers and pulling up survey stakes. But in the minds of some of the crazies, the APEs specifically, that meant something else. They began writing him letters, by way of their leader whose name I have forgotten but seem to recall it as being some kind of cheese like Liederkranz or Limburger or

Loubitelski or something (although maybe it did not start with an L) and telling him how much they agreed with his philosophies and methods and all. This turned out to be a load of road apples, but we did not know who they were at the time. So naturally, flattered from the bottom of his feet to the top of his swelled head, Dog-Nose goes and invites them up against my advice, for I did not see how his affiliation with some bunch of bulldozer-sitters could possibly facilitate our own objectives, as it were.

So up they come, a group of five, and it is clear from the instant of their arrival that this cheese-named character is playing with only about nine or ten checkers. He is, in his appearance, the vision of innocence and charity, like one of those people I have seen in white shirts and briefcases going door to door with the Word of God but whom you cannot remove from your doorstep, once they get you to answer your door, with any more ease than you can remove an entrenched tick from your scalp. This fellow, too, with his black-rimmed glasses and shirt-pocket full of pens, has that freshly-washed face of the religious zealot and that far-away look of bliss and peace that is supposed to be the result of having seen the Light but what I have found, whenever I have taken the time to talk to one of them, to be nothing more than a bunch of sanctimonious dogma they have memorized to fill their cavernous lack of intellect.

As I said, this fellow *looked* like one of that type, but he did not *sound* like one. And although he appeared cherubic and

harmless, and where his letters had been gentle and full of sensitive thoughts, his voice was like the hiss of a snake and his talk
was of destruction. His stimulus seemed to come largely from the
book of Revelations, and I could not help but think about Meyer
the Tyer and his peculiar, violent, but private worship of God. It
was becoming clear that the Bible, as my dear mother always
maintained, certainly did offer something for everyone who was
willing to look into it.

Well, this bunch wasted no time at revealing their true
nature and trying to convert Dog-Nose to the idea that his
"naive and impotent, kid-glove approach to the atrocity," as
Provolone or Mozzarella or whatever his name was put it, was
worthless and that their method of blowing up construction
sites, sniping at workers, and kidnapping developers was the
only recourse.

"We, alone, are the answer," says Roquefort, unfolding a
stack of dog-eared news clippings from his pack. "We are the
only ones to have ever stopped, for even a single day, the vile
and resolute advance of greed in the form of these filthy rapists,"
he hisses, waving the papers in our faces like they were the
tablets from the mountain, and I notice that he seems to be at
the mercy of his own eyebrows when he talks. Normally they are
hidden behind the thick black rims of his glasses, but whenever
he says anything, they each have an unnerving way of jumping
out from behind the rims like small bats that are trying to escape
from having their feet held by something.

While he rants on, we look at what those clippings report and see that this bunch is credited with enough violent acts to make a demolition derby seem like a Sunday ride in the country. They have dynamited a half-finished shopping center that was being built on some environmentally sensitive wetland, and they have stalled the work on an industrial complex for over a week by sniping at the machinery operators until they refused to show up for work. There was another batch of items about them holding some project manager hostage for three days until he agreed to a new environmental impact study on some other shopping mall that was being built over a swamp, and on and on, describing a real Bonnie and Clyde rampage of terrorism in Massachusetts and Rhode Island over the past few months. Here were some busy little campers all right.

Meanwhile, Port Salut is still ranting about the righteousness of their mission and the justification of their methodology, all the while punctuating his rhetoric with violent stabs to a birch log with a Bowie knife the size of a machete as his eyebrows jump around like crickets. His followers are entranced, and seem to be feeding his fervor by producing some kind of weird moaning sound in chorus, which sounds like the howls of a faraway pack of wolves carried on a night wind. My hair felt like it was standing up all over my back.

"Here, however, is the devil incarnate," spits Monterey Jack as one eyebrow, alone, flutters wildly over his glasses, the other one having apparently been beaten to death by the survivor. And he hands us a bigger clipping that features a photograph of a well-dressed fat guy cutting a ribbon at a construction site. The caption under the picture says he is a fellow by the name of Kronic Halitosis and that he has just begun construction on a large mall somewhere in New Hampshire.

"This son of a bitch," continues Parmesan, accompanied by the demonic drone and the crackling of the campfire that imparts a red glow to his face, "is singlehandedly responsible for the draining and filling of more wetlands, environmental laws be damned, than any other individual or group since the heyday of the Army Corps of Engineers. He makes a point of plowing over DEQE roadblocks by greasing the palms of politicians and making fallacious assurances that all concerns will be addressed and rectified. Yet, in the end, he has yet to respect the environmental laws, even in the most token regard, even once in any of his projects, and he leaves in his wake a barren wasteland of concrete and blacktop at the total expense of vital habitat. He scorns those who object to his unbridled greed and runs roughshod over their laws. No one has yet been able to even slow him down. Until us."

And with that he breaks out into a satanic laugh that The Shadow would have envied, and the rest of his troop join in with a bedlam of insane shrieking like a flock of hysterical gulls on a garbage heap.

"You've confronted this Halitosis fellow?" says Dog-Nose to Gorgonzola.

"Not yet," he croaks back, the rest of the group suddenly cackling like chickens, and the dead eyebrow resurrected now to join its companion in a frantic flight of celebration, "but we have made plans. You see, if we have learned nothing else from our experience at environmental terrorism, it is that one must never negotiate with these greed-driven development types. The project manager we held hostage agreed to our terms, and then nothing became of it. No, sir, we no longer will make deals. Our days of subtlety are passed. This time we will be more direct. We are going to kill Halitosis and blow up every one of his projects, both those in progress and those in use. No more deals."

The chorus had turned into the sound of keening, and in the night woods that surrounded us, I thought I felt the spirits of the dead brush past our camp, although I am not normally one to believe in such things.

Other than Jarlsberg himself, the other four members of the APEs were as tight-lipped as a horned pout, except for the background effects. None of them said anything, asked any questions, nor even spoke among themselves as far as I could tell. Their leader had absolute authority as far as the rest were concerned. The rest, by the way were composed of two men and two women, the latter of which were of such homely aspects (and I am being ridiculously magnanimous here) that even Dog-Nose was not moved to take his usual course with either of them. And that is saying something. But before I continue I should say that the males, too, were among the ugliest individuals I have ever come across on the daylight side of a rotted log, so I do not want to be seeing any grousing letters from the ladies about my being unkind to their gender. Fair is fair.

"So you're planning to perpetrate the most infamous act of environmental terrorism the world has yet seen," says Dog-Nose, clearly disenchanted with the caliber and philosophical bent of this band of APEs. "And just what is it that you want from me?"

The chorus instantly changes to the sound of a church choir, highs and lows and harmonic intricacies all blending into a symphonic resonance that would seem impossible to produce with only four voices. And Ricotta spits in his reptilian sibilance, "Don't be condescending. We want your blessing," a wide, thin-lipped grin spreading flat across his face, and the eyebrows beating in unison, like two dire crows rowing across a gray winter sky.

"Over my dead body!" I begin to shout just as Dog-Nose's boot tip catches me under the armpit, knocking me out of my chair, and what comes out instead is something that sounded more like, "Over my de......hhhhuuuugaaarrrrrugghh-hhoooooffshiiiiit!" And before I can scream "What the hell did you do that for?" I hear Dog-Nose saying, "How about letting me sleep on it?"

"Sure," hisses Havarti, his eyebrows seeming to do a shuffley little soft shoe across the stage of his forehead. And we all go into our separate tents to do just that.

Not wanting to take any chances at being overheard, Dog-Nose proceeds to scribbling me a note almost the second we get out of sight of the APEs, the gist of which was that we might well wake up to find our throats cut from ear to ear if we are not extremely careful about how we handle this crowd, and it is in our best interest to not show these loonies what we really think of them. Furthermore, Dog-Nose relays to me, we may already be in a seriously dangerous predicament, and he would appreciate my not flying off the handle and squishing all the eggshells we are now walking on. I think this over for about two seconds and make exactly five sign-language gestures at him: a ring with my thumb and forefinger, a poke at him with my pointer, a thumb in the direction of the APEs's tent, a poke at myself, and a hand-waving signal like an umpire makes to show that a runner is safe. He was supposed to take that as meaning, "Okay, but you handle *them*. I want nothing to do with this." I believe he got the message, for he made an unmistakable gesture back.

To our surprise and relief, we were both still alive the next morning, but unfortunately, so were the APEs. Now it was just a matter of waiting to see how Dog-Nose was going to handle the situation, and although I was not usually one to leave such things in his hands without some two-cents-worth of my opinion, in this case I really was at a total loss for knowing what to do or say that would not run the risk of setting off some kind of ugly incident. Meanwhile I have remembered the guy's name and find to my embarrassment that it was not a cheese at all but a kind of beer— Lowenbrau— which is why I originally thought of Liederkranz. It is an honest mistake.

So Lowenbrau is already awake and sitting by the fire (which I am surprised to see that he has started and has set a pot of coffee to boiling, as well) and is honing his outsized knife as he looks up with his pale eyes that almost look goat-like in the grey light of morning. The others are nowhere to be seen.

"Sleep on it?" he says to Dog-Nose. And as I look at Dog-Nose I can see in his face that he has not slept at all.

"Yes, I have," lies Dog-Nose. "I've decided that if it's simply my blessing you want, not support, not endorsement, not aid, and if you will clear out immediately so that we can get on with our own business, I'll give it. If there are any strings, though, we'll have to discuss it."

I was shocked, like a brick had hit my stomach from the inside. I knew Dog-Nose could not possibly support these lunatics, and I was equally sure that saying he did, even to save our skins, must have been a terribly painful decision for him, though probably not nearly as painful as dying. Still, I knew Dog-Nose to be a highly moral individual when it came to matters of principle (sometimes to the point of being a real obstinate asshole about things that I could not see the importance of at all), and for him to kowtow to this pack of slime-balls was something mighty alarming.

"No strings," grins Lowenbrau, his fluttering eyebrows seeming to suddenly fold in upon themselves and disappear behind his glasses as though into the mouth of a cave. And at the instant the words leave his smirking lips, the sound of automatic weapons being snapped back on safety and a hum like the sound of a tree full of contented bees emanates from the woods all around us.

Into camp step the four APEs we knew about, followed by over a dozen more who had been hiding in the surrounding forest, all armed to the hilt with M-16s, grenades, and a whole arsenal of U.S. Army surplus weaponry.

Me and Dog-Nose look at each other like we have just stepped onto solid ground after crossing a deep gorge on a rope bridge, just as the bridge crumbles into the gorge behind us. It was horribly clear that the wrong reaction would have us filled with more holes than a Mafia alibi. For me, the sunny summer morning turned as damp and cool as a November evening, even though it still looked the same, and as the army of APEs wordlessly packed up their gear and faded off into the woods, accompanied by a high buzzing whine like an electric power line just before a thunder storm, I knew something fundamental had changed.

It was written in the tired eyes and tensed jawline of Dog-Nose's face. The celebrity game had showed its real dark side, finally. We had glimpsed it a few times, as I have written, but here it was standing naked and ugly in front of us—too many crazies with too many claws, too much at stake for too little esteem. Pieces of the Legend were getting too valuable. Where injury once could come from a false step, now death could come from a false word. Dog-Nose looked like the game had lost its shine. I believe he felt the November evening, too.

"The equation is too far out of balance, lately," Dog-Nose said to me later that day. "Imagine anyone placing equal value on two lives, yours and mine, and on my simply saying 'Yes, I support your cause,' even knowing full well that I didn't mean it. An empty, valueless testimony equals two human lives. I expend more thought and emotion each time I kill a fish."

In the following weeks, we read a great deal about the APEs, who had taken to calling themselves the Dog-Nose Brigade of the Alliance for Preservation of the Environment, thus necessitating my sending off a slew of press releases on Dog-Nose's behalf denying any endorsement, connection, knowledge, or sanction of the activities of any group whatsoever, including the Audubon Society, Cub Scouts, and American Heart Association.

But those APEs were raising some hell on a regional scale, and the more I read about the acquisitive tactics of that arrogant bastard, Halitosis, the more I found myself rooting for the APEs in an ambivalent kind of way. To tell the honest truth, my ideal scenario was to have the APEs and Halitosis blow themselves up together, thus ridding the world of two forms of demon that it can better do without. But of course things do not go so neatly. In fact, what happened, as you probably remember, is that most of the APEs got killed or arrested in a well-publicized shootout with the authorities during a raid on their so-called bomb factory shortly after they dynamited the Head of the Sphinx Mall on the 20th of December 1968, killing and injuring hundreds of Christmas shoppers. Halitosis, himself, was supposed to have been there to preside over the Grand Opening of his mall, which had finally been completed after unprecedented disregard for the highly sensitive nature of the wetland upon which it was built, but he decided to fly to the Bahamas instead. Lowenbrau and a couple of others escaped and effectively disappeared. It is believed that Lowenbrau himself went so far as to get a face-change and sex-change operation, so for all I know he could be my landlady.

Halitosis is still murdering the environment and lying to authorities and disregarding laws meant to keep self-indulgent shitheads from doing any of that. And, of course, he is getting richer than God and laughing all the way to the bank. Maybe Meyer is right. Maybe God lets that type get away with such things because they are the ones most closely created in His image. I cannot believe I have just written that but, having done so, I will leave it be, just to show you how sad a turn things had taken.

It was soon after these events that we began to intentionally wind down the celebrity aspect of our business. I had achieved the goal I had set out to achieve—that of making Dog-Nose into a Legend in his own time—and Dog-Nose had achieved the notoriety he wanted, once it was clear that it was not going to be too hard to get. And so, easy come, easy go, we let the hoopla settle back down with the summer dust and resumed our quiet lives, guiding the occasional client, helping the local authorities when someone or something had to be tracked, and taking it easy enjoying those activities that had, after so many years of being considered work, lost their appeal as simple pleasures. And it was not long after that that Dog-Nose met his unfortunate end, just as you have read it in the original magazine article that is now Chapter 1.

To end this chapter, and the book as well, I have found something in the box that seems appropriate. I know Dog-Nose wrote it shortly after the APEs incident, and it shows his disenchantment with the whole guiding business like nothing else he ever wrote. In some ways, it is kind of funny and comical, but you should not be fooled by that. To me, it is obvious that it is what we authors call metaphoric, because I know his state of mind and the surrounding events when he wrote it.

But before I show you that piece, I would like to say good-bye and thank you for reading all this. I hope you now have a better idea of how things were with the so-called legendary Dog-Nose Cooper. It was not exactly a pleasure to write this book, but it seemed to me that it had to be done, and maybe it will make me a buck or two. Here's the piece:

BIG TWO-FISTED RIVER—PART I

Nick crawled out from under the pack. He had asked the baggage man to toss his pack off the train when they reached the river. He had not meant while he was wearing it and he had not meant this river. He crawled out from under the pack. The river he was trying to reach was still two hundred miles away. Nick would have to walk, the heavy pack hanging from his shoulders like a dead bull.

It was hard going. Nick stopped after three days and smoked a cigarette. He slipped the bull-heavy pack from his shoulders and propped it against a stump. The going had been hard. There was plenty more hard going to go. Nick did not mind because the going had been the hardness of good going. He smoked his cigarette. He thought of the whores he had met at the railway station.

Nick stood up and shouldered his pack. Now it felt like two dead bulls but Nick felt good. He had only another hundred miles to go. As he walked he thought of the trout. Then he thought of how good he felt and of how good it would feel to fight the trout, knee deep in the river. In the pack were his cape, his muleta, and his sword. Nick carried in his hand the leather case that held the banderillos. Nick remembered how good it was to fight the trout, long ago on the Bull River.

He had been good with the cape, the trout responding well to his veronicas and final recorte. He always lured the big trout from their deep holes along the banks with the cape. Then Nick placed the banderillos. He placed them well, arching over the fish as the big trout made its upstream rush. Then he mastered the trout with the muleta. He made the trout lower its head. Each time the trout charged the muleta it bled from the banderillos. The bleeding brought its head down. Then, facing the trout, Nick drew the sword from the muleta. He rose to his toes, sighting down the sword, and thrust the sword into

162

the fish; a clean kill. The sword entered the trout behind the head, the point slitting the belly from vent to jaw. They were all good trout, killed and cleaned in one stroke, all the insides coming out together, the ears and tail in one piece. It would be that way again soon. The old feelings were returning. Nick thought of fighting trout on the Bull a long time ago and of how he would soon be fighting trout again because he was nearing the river.

After three more days Nick reached the river. He was too tired to do anything. He was too tired to pitch a tent. He was too tired to build a fire. He was too tired to cook dinner. Two hundred miles is a long walk, Nick thought. He was too tired to fight trout. Nick got out a bottle of whiskey. He leaned back against the trunk of a pine and drank the bottle of whiskey. He was too tired to screw the top back on so he finished the whole bottle of whiskey. It was not very good whiskey but he had carried it and the rest of the case for two hundred miles.

Nick opened another bottle. He struck a match on the side of his nose and lit a cigarette. There would be plenty of days to fight the trout.

10
THE REVELATION

She can dance a Cajun rhythm,
Jump like a Willy's in 4-wheel-drive.
She's a summer love in the spring, fall, and winter.
She can make happy any man alive.

— The Grateful Dead

I have decided to write this last chapter even though it was the last thing in my mind when I started this project. In fact this whole book and the writing of it were for the exact opposite purpose from the thing I am now about to reveal. But that is the way things come out sometimes, and I have found that there are a lot of things in life that work in just that way, so even though I am about as surprised as meeting a skunk in the outhouse on a dark night for telling what I am about to tell, I am not so surprised.

It all came about when I thought I was finished with the book, which was when I concluded the last chapter that you just read before this one. I pulled the last sheet out of the typewriter and shuffled all the pages together that had come to be a pile of some heft, and I hunkered down and began reading what I had written. And when I came to the end and sat back with a huge sigh of relief and a general feeling of self-satisfaction at having done a fine job of what I set out to do, I thought about Dog-Nose's wife and about how it had been her encouragement that set this whole thing off and running, and how it behooved me to let her have a look at how it had gone.

So I sent her off a Xerox copy of the manuscript, and before I get any smartass letters from somebody about how I am improperly using a trade name for a generic term, let me get straight right now as to how the copy I made to send to the lady was the genuine article that was actually made on a machine manufactured by the Xerox company. I bring that up on account of an ordeal that was precipitated some time back by an article Dog-Nose wrote in which he had mentioned something about using Scotch tape to do an emergency fix on a fly reel (or maybe that was part of one of those phoney press releases I wrote myself— I am not too sure) and how it commenced a whole hubub that I do not wish to go into right now.

So I sent her a copy of the manuscript, and I waited ten days, and in came a letter with the familiar penmanship that was the first thing I noticed about her other letter that started the whole thing. When I open the envelope and unfold the stationery, the waft of lily-of-the-valley hits my nose about the same exact instant as the two words in curly ink letters hit my eyes, and I fall back into my chair about as close to fainting as I have ever come since the kerosene heater went haywire one night when I was a kid and sucked all the air out of my room. The two words went fuzzy for a while, came back all broken up into a patch of white spots that looked like a swarm of gnats against the sky, swung around the page a half a dozen times, and finally settled down where they had started and stared at me like a skull. "Come home" was all they said, and I knew the jig was up.

What jig?

The pretense that I was Junior Fraser and that Westlake Coleridge "Dog-Nose" Cooper was dead.

What did she suspect?

She did not "suspect." She knew.

Knew what?

That I was alive.

I who?

Wes Cooper a.k.a. Westlake Coleridge Cooper a.k.a. W.C. Cooper a.k.a. Outhouse Cooper a.k.a. Dog-Nose Cooper.

Then who is Ishmael "Junior" Fraser?

He was my partner who was supposed to have wrote this book and in whose name I have wrote it.

But he did not write the book?

No.

Who did?

Me.

And the admission is being made here and now that the jig is up and that Dog-Nose Cooper, not Junior Fraser, actually wrote all of the preceding?

Yes.

Then why are you still writing in the argot of an unedu-cated rustic?

I'm sorry. After all this time, it's hard to break out of the persona.

Don't you think you had better tell us all about it?

That is my intention.

When?

Yes I suppose Ill have to do some explaining sooner or later I knew the charade was over the moment I opened her let-ter and saw the words come home centered in her flowing cur-sive on the page they struck me like the sight of my own grave-stone but soon became soft and beckoning as the scent of her perfume and the slender tendrils of the writing took hold of my senses and eased the shock I knew it was all over but it didnt seem to matter any more her simple message was like an embrace that Ive been waiting to feel for more than a score of years and she knew all along somehow which is the most amaz-ing thing I see now that she suspected since the publication of the article that became the first chapter and thats why she sent the box and coaxed me to continue knowing that the more I wrote the more she could verify her suspicion and I found later in fact that what certified it for her was the fact that she knew the contents of that box of writing better than I did and when I included a couple of poems in the text that Id composed during the writing of this book she knew that they hadnt been written previously and that junior wasnt writing the book yes she is an extraordinary woman and our mutual love has survived a fusillade of outrageous fortune entirely from a front I led myself I dont know what wildness had hold of me in the early years but its a rare mate with a singular and deep affection who can summon the patience sympathy and love to endure I took callous advantage of it gallivanting around the northeast wearing the oncebright cloak of notoriety until it began to weigh heavily on my shoulders after a while it seemed that every crackpot cause and halfassed celebrityhunter wanted a piece of the legend and yes it became very old junior had done his work well we lived like kings for the most part but after 12 years enough became more than enough when he drowned I saw it as the perfect opportunity to sneak quietly off into reclusiveness and leaked a story to the press that the great Dog-Nose Cooper had disappeared unfortunately those two assholes Baker and Gilroy began investigating as research for their insipid book and I was forced to bury myself even deeper to avoid their prying after the book if I can use the term without insulting the entire body of world literature came out I realized that if I didnt put an end to uncertainty about the fate of Dog-Nose Cooper it wouldnt be long before every twobit reporter and outdoor journalist would be turning over every brushpile and poking into every cave in North America to find out what happened to the legend and whether I was alive so I wrote that original article entitled for the record and had it published in one of the better outdoor magazines assuming the persona of junior and attempting to settle the dust once and for all I have little doubt that the plan was sound except for the unforeseen devotion and uncanny perspicacity of one Molly Bea Rothschild Cooper aka Mrs Westlake Coleridge Cooper who saw the handwriting on the wall as though my own signature appeared at the bottom of it and I never saw the box she sent for the tender trap that it was I thought too I had done a masterful job of mixing the proper amount of self denigration with hubris from the standpoint of junior to make it seem an authentic product of his authorship and Molly Bea heaped great praise upon me for the virtuosity I displayed in the deception no one but she could have possibly known the difference and even she freely admits would now still be in some doubt had I not included pieces not from the box but with the trap sprung I could do nothing but accept her invitation indeed did not want to do anything but accept it hoping only that the warmth and consolation with which I had endowed those two swirls of ink truly expressed the emotions of their author I

could easily have misread them thinking them to have a soft-
ness like feather bedding warm comforting like the home to
which one can always return no matter how far one has strayed
but they could equally have held in their pigment the conde-
scension of the wronged but patient partner the resignation of
one who feels martyred by the fate of having wed a wayward
child bearing up under the soothing balm of sanctimony an
adherent of the regrettable philosophy that boys will be boys I
knew that was not it that was not my Molly Bea for whom the
love I had held from her for these many years enormous and
profound as it was had been not wasted nor dispersed nor
squandered upon others despite my wellpublicized escapades
which were nothing but hormonal glandular drives body parts
and the blending of excretions to which I fully confess a pen-
chant but which have little to do with sincerity or even fidelity
yes the bond shared with Molly Bea is galactic in dimension
and like a collapsing star it had condensed tighter and smaller
and denser and blacker within me until its entirety took up no
more space than a gallstone heavy as the sun and burning it was
all still there to be given back to her take it in your hand if it
does not kill you plant it in your heart and nurture it like a
child let us watch it grow once more giggling and fat filled with
life and health and its breath fragrant with milk and innocence
to sanctify our lives I wanted to run to her right away and I did
driving all day to the almost forgotten address and I didnt get
halfway up the brick walk in the charcoal gray evening when

the door opened and she stood there silhouetted against the warm light spilling out behind her onto the brick path smiling out at me knowing I was coming at that moment the winter evening cold and the Christmas shoppers crunching along the icy sidewalks stopping on their way home from work in the shops of Harvard Square sleighbells from a sidewalk Santa jingling off in the distance like a chorus of spring peepers in the glowing streetlights I could see her breath on the cold air and the calm smile behind it until the tears filled my eyes and the black stone reversed its contraction in a sudden upwelling that crushed me in waves of unbearable serenity a violence of tranquility and peace that brought me to my knees I could feel the cold of the bricks through my pantlegs as I sobbed there and the sudden gentle touch that led me into the warmth of the house shaking Wes she said welcome back with her arms around my neck and I held her my wet cheeks pressed against her neck silent with no idea what to say to her knowing that there may in fact be no words to suffice in any event except the warmth that flowed between our bodies she lifted her head and kissed the tears from the side of my cheek and along my chin our mouths in search of each other and in the depths of our kiss she drew me into the room and down upon the soft rug in front of the blazing fireplace I found the opening in her robe and felt a skin the unique smoothness of which I had forgotten and the tears welled up again as she helped me out of my coat and the rest of my clothes and as we lay together before the fire sealed once more in an embrace that fit like Incan stonework and our mouths and hands moved upon the surfaces of each others bodies O God I was filled with her scent and a remorse so overpowering that her breasts were awash with my tears O her hands ravishing my body as though Lord she were trying to assimilate me into herself myself herself and as I ran my tongue down between those soft mounds and the fire crackling as the logs shifted themselves and settling into a better fit sparks spraying like fiery seafoam yes I asked her if she would forgive me Wes she said I have always forgiven you yes I asked her if I could stay forever and she asked is that what you want to do I suddenly realized with a clarity as limpid as the eyes of a cat that that was what I wanted to do no matter what was likely to transpire from the revelations published herein and I said yes if you will let me and she took hold of my poor overworked balls in a grip of iron that had waited twentyfive years and Wes she said Wes I will Wes.